MW00451247

MATH
INSTANT ASSESSMENTS
for Data Tracking
Grade 4

Credits
Author: Natalie Rompella

Visit *carsondellosa.com* for correlations to Common Core, state, national, and Canadian provincial standards.

Carson-Dellosa Publishing, LLC
PO Box 35665
Greensboro, NC 27425 USA
carsondellosa.com

978-1-4838-3612-6
01-339161151

Table of Contents

✦ Assessment and Data Tracking ✦

Data tracking is an essential element in modern classrooms. Teachers are often required to capture student learning through both formative and summative assessments. They then must use the results to guide teaching, remediation, and lesson planning and provide feedback to students, parents, and administrators. Because time is always at a premium in the classroom, it is vital that teachers have the assessments they need at their fingertips. The assessments need to be suited to the skill being assessed as well as adapted to the stage in the learning process. This is true for an informal checkup at the end of a lesson or a formal assessment at the end of a unit.

This book will provide the tools and assessments needed to determine your students' level of mastery throughout the school year. The assessments are both formal and informal and include a variety of formats—pretests and posttests, flash cards, prompt cards, traditional tests, and exit tickets. Often, there are several assessment options for a single skill or concept to allow you the greatest flexibility when assessing understanding. Simply select the assessment that best fits your needs, or use them all to create a comprehensive set of assessments for before, during, and after learning.

Incorporate Instant Assessments into your daily plans to streamline the data-tracking process and keep the focus on student mastery and growth.

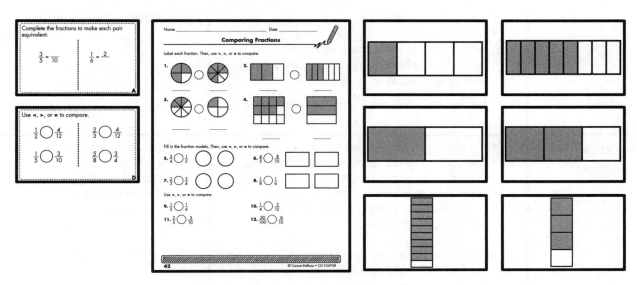

A variety of instant assessments for comparing fractions

Types of Assessment

Assessment usually has a negative association because it brings to mind tedious pencil-and-paper tests and grading. However, it can take on many different forms and be a positive, integral part of the year. Not all assessments need to be formal, nor do they all need to be graded. Choose the type of assessment to use based on the information you need to gather. Then, you can decide if or how it should be graded.

	What Does It Look Like?	**Examples**
Formative Assessment	• occurs during learning • is administered frequently • is usually informal and not graded • identifies areas of improvement • provides immediate feedback so a student can make adjustments promptly, if needed • allows teachers to rethink strategies, lesson content, etc., based on current student performance • is process-focused • has the most impact on a student's performance	• in-class observations • exit tickets • reflections and journaling • homework • student-teacher conferences • student self-evaluations
Interim Assessment	• occurs occasionally • is more formal and usually graded • feedback is not immediate, though still fairly quick • helps teachers identify gaps in teaching and areas for remediation • often includes performance assessments, which are individualized, authentic, and performance-based in order to evaluate higher-level thinking skills	• in-class observations • exit tickets • reflections and journaling • homework • student-teacher conferences • student self-evaluations
Summative Assessment	• occurs once learning is considered complete • the information is used by the teacher and school for broader purposes • takes time to return a grade or score • can be used to compare a student's performance to others • is product-focused • has the least impact on a student's performance since there are few or no opportunities for retesting	• cumulative projects • final portfolios • quarterly testing • end-of-the-year testing • standardized testing

How to Use This Book

The assessments in this book follow a few different formats, depending on the skill or concept being assessed. Use the descriptions below to familiarize yourself with each unique format and get the most out of Instant Assessments all year long.

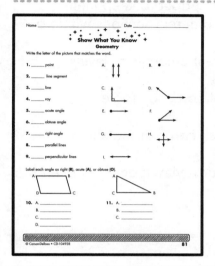

Show What You Know

Each domain begins with a pair of *Show What You Know* tests. Both tests follow the same format and include the same types of questions so they can be directly compared to show growth. Use them as a pretest and posttest. Or, use one as a test at the end of a unit and use the second version as a retest for students after remediation.

Exit Tickets

Each domain ends with exit tickets that cover the variety of concepts within the domain. Exit tickets are very targeted questions designed to assess understanding of specific skills, so they are ideal formative assessments to use at the end of a lesson. Exit tickets do not have space for student names, allowing teachers to gather information on the entire class without placing pressure on individual students. If desired, have students write their names or initials on the backs of the tickets. Other uses for exit tickets include the following:

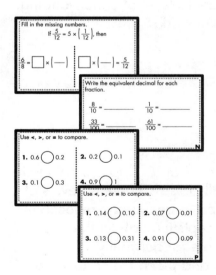

- Use the back of each ticket for longer answers, fuller explanations, or extension questions. If needed, students can staple them to larger sheets of paper.
- They can also be used for warm-ups or to find out what students know before a lesson.
- Use the generic exit tickets on pages 7 and 8 for any concept you want to assess. Be sure to fill in any blanks before copying.
- Laminate them and place them in a math center as task cards.
- Use them to play Scoot or a similar review game at the end of a unit.
- Choose several to create a targeted assessment for a skill or set of skills.

Cards

Use the cards as prompts for one-on-one conferencing. Simply copy the cards, cut them apart, and follow the directions preceding each set of cards. Use the lettering to keep track of which cards a student has interacted with.

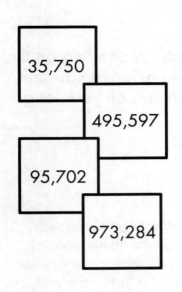

- Copy on card stock and/or laminate for durability.
- Punch holes in the top left corners and place the cards on a book ring to make them easily accessible.
- Copy the sets on different colors of paper to keep them easily separated or to distinguish different sections within a set of cards.
- Easily differentiate by using different amounts or levels of cards to assess a student.
- Write the answers on the backs of cards to create self-checking flash cards.
- Place them in a math center as task cards or matching activities.
- Use them to play Scoot or a similar review game at the end of a unit.

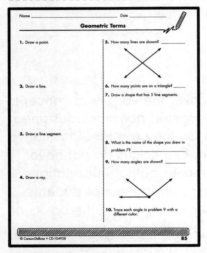

Assessment Pages

The reproducible assessment pages are intended for use as a standard test of a skill. Use them in conjunction with other types of assessment to get a full picture of a student's level of understanding. They can also be used for review or homework.

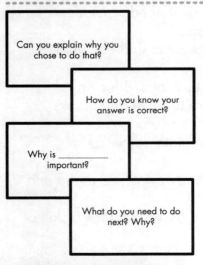

Math Talk Prompt Cards

Use the math talk prompt cards on pages 9 and 10 to prompt math discussions that can be used to informally assess students' levels of understanding. Use the math talk prompts to encourage reflection and deeper understanding of math concepts throughout the year.

- Copy on card stock and/or laminate for durability.
- Punch holes in the top left corners and place the cards on a book ring to keep them easily accessible.
- Use them for journaling prompts.
- Place them in a math center to be used with other activities.

Exit Tickets

Exit tickets are a useful formative assessment tool that you can easily work into your day. You can choose to use a single exit ticket at the end of the day, or at the end of each lesson. Simply choose a ticket below, make one copy for each student, and have students complete the prompt and present them to you as their ticket out of the door. Use the student responses to gauge overall learning, make small remediation groups, or target areas for reteaching. A blank exit ticket is included on page 8 so you can create your own exit tickets as well.

What stuck with you today? _____ _____ _____ _____ _____	List three facts you learned today. Put them in order from most important to least important. _____ _____ _____ _____
The first thing I'll tell my family about today is _____ _____ _____ _____ .	The most important thing I learned today is _____ _____ _____ _____ _____ .
Color the face that shows how you feel about understanding today's lesson. ☺ 😐 ☹ Explain why. _____ _____	Summarize today's lesson in 10 words or less. _____ _____ _____ _____

One example of _____ is _____

_____

_____

_____

_____ .

One question I still have is _____

_____

_____

_____

_____ .

How will understanding _____

_____

help you in real life? _____

_____

_____

_____

One new word I learned today is _____

_____ .

It means _____

_____

_____ .

Draw a picture related to the lesson. Add a caption.

_____

_____

If today's lesson were a song, the title would

be _____

_____

because _____

_____ .

The answer is _____ .

What is the question? _____

_____

_____

_____

Use these prompts when observing individual students in order to better understand their thinking and depth of understanding of a concept. These cards may also be used during whole-class lessons or in small remediation groups to encourage students to explain their thinking with different concepts.

How did you solve it?	What strategy did you use?
How could you solve it a different way?	Can you repeat that in your own words?
Explain your thinking.	Did you use any key words? Which ones?

Can you explain why you chose to do that?	Why did you choose to add/subtract/ multiply/divide?
How do you know your answer is correct?	How can you prove your answer?
Is this like any other problems you have solved? How?	What would change if . . .?
Why is _____ important?	What do you need to do next? Why?

Name _____ Date _____

✦ Show What You Know ✦
Operations and Algebraic Thinking

Write the related multiplication equation for each word problem. Then, solve.

1. Daniela is 9 years old. Her mother is 4 times older. How old is her mother?

_____

2. Luke has 4 pencils. His sister has 5 times as many. How many pencils does his sister have?

_____

3. Write a word problem that compares two amounts for the following equation.

$$4 \times 8 = 32$$

_____

_____

4. Write the related equation. Then, solve. Show your work.

Mrs. Garcia's class is collecting canned food to donate to the local food pantry. Last year, they collected 1,435 cans. They want to beat that number this year. If they have collected 764 so far, how many more do they need to collect to reach last year's amount?

Write the equation. _____

5. Draw as many different kinds of arrays as you can for the number 6. Below each array, write the related multiplication problem.

Factors of 6: _____

6. Is 6 prime or composite? _____

How do you know? _____

_____

7. Write the first eight multiples of 4: _____

_____

Write the first eight multiples of 6: _____

_____

Circle the multiples the two numbers have in common.

8. Beginning with 2, add 6. Find the next four numbers in the pattern.

2, _____, _____, _____, _____

✦ Show What You Know ✦
Operations and Algebraic Thinking

Write the related multiplication equation for each word problem. Then, solve.

1. Aaliyah weighs 40 pounds. Her dad weighs 5 times as much. How much does her dad weigh?

_____

2. Mrs. Webber bought 3 bananas at the grocery store. She bought 4 times as many tangerines. How many tangerines did she buy?

_____

3. Write a word problem that compares two amounts for the following equation.

$$7 \times 8 = 56$$

_____

_____

4. Write the related equation. Then, solve. Show your work.

Baseball cards come in packs of 11 cards. Luke and Mia own 6 packs of cards between them. How many cards do they have between the two of them?

Write the equation. _____

If they each own the same number of cards, how many cards does each own? _____

5. Draw as many different kinds of arrays as you can for the number 20. Below each array, write the multiplication problem.

Factors of 20: _____

6. Is 20 prime or composite? _____

How do you know? _____

_____

7. Write the first eight multiples of 3: _____

_____

Write the first eight multiples of 8: _____

_____

Circle the multiples the two numbers have in common.

8. Beginning with 2, multiply by 2 and subtract 1. Find the next four numbers in the pattern.

2, _____, _____, _____, _____

Multiplication Equations

Write the related multiplication equation for each word problem.

1. Ava is 4 years old. Her sister is 3 times older. How old is her sister?

_____

2. Jose picked up 12 sticks in his backyard. His father picked up 4 times as many. How many sticks did his father pick up?

_____

3. How many fingers are there on 6 hands?

_____

4. There are 48 total slices of pie. If each pie has 6 slices, how many pies are there?

_____

5. Lucy has $6. Her older brother has 6 times that amount. How much money does her brother have?

_____

Write a word problem that compares two amounts for the following equations.

6. $7 \times 3 = 21$

_____

_____

7. $11 \times 4 = 44$

_____

_____

8. $5 \times 12 = 60$

_____

_____

Name _____ Date _____

Word Problems

Write the related equation. Then, solve. Show your work.

1. Mrs. Clement bought a bag of candy for her daughter's party. It contains 60 pieces of candy. There will be 7 children at the party. If she wants to give an equal amount to each child, how many pieces of candy will each child get?

Write the equation. _____

How many pieces will be left over? _____

2. Ella owns 7 pairs of shoes. Her sister owns 4 pairs of shoes. How many total shoes do they have?

Write the equation. _____

3. The Fire soccer team is having a pizza celebration. Each child will get 3 slices. Each pizza has 8 slices. If there are 10 children on the team, how many pizzas do they need to order?

Write the equation. _____

Why? _____

_____

4. Ben wants to read 200 minutes a week. He read 20 minutes on Sunday. If he reads every day for the rest of the week, how many minutes will he need to read each day to reach 200 minutes?

Write the equation. _____

5. The art teacher needs to buy paper. Each student will need 5 sheets. There are 23 students in the class. There are 100 sheets of paper sold in a pack. How many packs of paper will she need to buy?

Write the equation. _____

Name _____   Date _____

Factors

Draw as many different arrays as you can for each number. Below each array, write the related multiplication problem. Then, list the factors.

1. 10

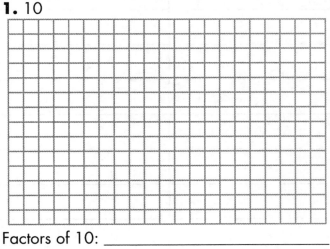

Factors of 10: _____

2. 13

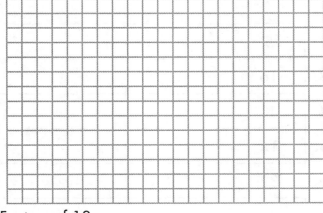

Factors of 13: _____

3. 2

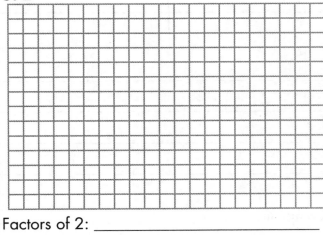

Factors of 2: _____

4. 12

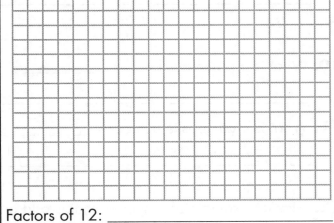

Factors of 12: _____

5. Choose one of the numbers above. Explain how the arrays are related to the number's factors.

_____

_____

6. List the factors of 8.

_____

Name _____ Date _____

Factors

Complete the chart.

	Number	Even or Odd?	Factors	Prime or Composite?
1.	2			
2.	5			
3.	16			
4.	40			
5.	17			
6.	32			
7.	45			
8.	27			
9.	24			

10. What is a prime number? _____

_____

11. What is a composite number? _____

_____

12. Give an example of a number that is odd and composite. _____

13. Give an example of a number that is even and prime. _____

14. Choose one of the three problems below. Explain why the answer is even or odd. _____

_____

_____

2 even	3 odd	2 even
+ 4 even	+ 5 odd	+ 5 odd
6 even	8 even	7 odd

Multiples

Complete each chart.

1.

Number	The First Eight Multiples	Common Multiples
2		
5		

2.

Number	The First Eight Multiples	Common Multiples
2		
3		

3.

Number	The First Eight Multiples	Common Multiples
5		
10		

4.

Number	The First Eight Multiples	Common Multiples
6		
20		

5.

Number	The First Eight Multiples	Common Multiples
7		
8		

Name _____ Date _____

Number Patterns

Fill in the missing numbers and operations.

	Pattern	Rule	Next Three Numbers in the Sequence
1.	3, 6, 9, 12, . . .	add [ ]	
2.	90, 82, 74, 66, . . .	[ ] 8	
3.	2, 9, 23, 51, . . .	multiply by 2 and add [ ]	
4.	3, 7, 15, 31, . . .	multiply by [ ] and add [ ]	
5.	1, 2, 4, 8, . . .		

Complete each pattern.

6. Beginning with 3, add 5.

3, _____, _____, _____, _____

7. Beginning with 40, subtract 7.

40, _____, _____, _____, _____

8. Beginning with 1, multiply by 3 and subtract 2.

1, _____, _____, _____, _____

9. ◯ , ▢ , △ , ☆ , ◯ , _____ , △

10. What would the 8th shape be in the pattern in problem 9? _____

How do you know? _____

_____

11. What would the 39th shape be? _____

How do you know? _____

_____

12. Look at problem 1. What do you notice about the pattern? _____

_____

A

Write the related multiplication equation.

The zoo has 3 giraffes. They have 8 times as many monkeys. How many monkeys are at the zoo?

_____

B

Write the related multiplication equation.

Dominic is making a fruit salad. He put in 4 strawberries. Then, he added 3 times as many grapes. How many grapes will be in his fruit salad?

_____

C

Write a word problem that compares two amounts for the following equation.

$$9 \times 3 = 27$$

_____

_____

_____

D

Write the related equation. Then, solve. Show your work.

A bakery makes 48 muffins a day. If the muffin tin holds 12 muffins, how many batches are made each day?

Write the equation. _____

E

Write the related equation. Then, solve. Show your work.

An egg carton holds 12 eggs. There are four cartons of eggs. How many eggs are there in all?

Write the equation. _____

F

List all of the multiplication problems with a product of 18.

Factors of 18: _____

G

List the factors of 24.

H

Circle the factors of 14.

1	2	3	4	5
6	7	8	9	10
11	12	13	14	15
16	17	18	19	20

Is 18 prime or composite? _____

How do you know? _____

_____

_____

_____

_____

I

Circle the prime numbers.

1	2	3	4	5
6	7	8	9	10
11	12	13	14	15
16	17	18	19	20

J

Circle the numbers that are both odd and composite.

11   12   15   16

21   24   25   28

K

Write the first eight multiples of 5.

_____

Write the first eight multiples of 6.

_____

Circle the multiple(s) the two numbers have in common.

L

Circle the multiple(s) 8 and 9 have in common.

18   24   32   36

40   48   54   63

64   72   81

M

What are the next four numbers in the pattern?

1, 4, 7, 10, _____, _____, _____, _____

What is the rule for the pattern?

_____

N

Beginning with 1, add 2 and multiply by 2. Find the next four numbers in the pattern.

1, _____, _____, _____, _____

O

Write the rule for the following pattern:

50, 102, 206, 414, ...

Multiply by _____ and _____.

How do you know? _____

_____

P

Name _____ Date _____

Number and Operations in Base Ten

Circle the correct answer.

1. 600 is (10, 100, 1,000) times larger than 60.

2. 100 is (10, 100, 1,000) times smaller than 10,000.

Solve.

3. 400 ÷ 40 = _____

4. 70 × 10,000 = _____

Write the value of the underlined digit.

5. 583,6<u>1</u>2 = _____

6. 9<u>0</u>1,826 = _____

7. Write the number in standard form.

five thousand six hundred twenty-six

_____

8. Circle the standard form.

900,000 + 4,000 + 700 + 10 + 6

947,716   904,716   94,716

9. Write in word form.

509,302

_____

_____

10. Round 248,503 to each place value.

hundreds _____

ten thousands _____

hundred thousands _____

tens _____

thousands _____

Use **<**, **>**, or **=** to compare.

11. 1,420 4,000

12. fifty-six thousand  6,500

13. 490,300 400,000 + 90,000 + 300

14. three hundred thousand ◯ 1,000,000

$$6 \quad 2 \quad 9 \quad 3$$

15. Build the largest whole number possible using the digits above. _____

16. Build the smallest whole number possible using the digits above. _____

17. Explain how you figured out the largest number possible. _____

_____

Add or subtract.

18.   862
        + 169

19.   521
        – 206

20.   10,000
       – 6,213

21.   83,863
        + 8,977

Multiply.

22.   62
          × 7

23.   9,384
          ×   6

24.   83
          × 41

25.   6,109
          ×   7

Divide. Show the remainder if there is one.

26. 6)42

27. 8)168

28. 3)41

29. 5)6,833

Name _____ Date _____

Show What You Know
Number and Operations in Base Ten

Circle the correct answer.

1. 8,000 is (10, 100, 1,000) times larger than 8.

2. 60 is (10, 100, 1,000) times smaller than 600.

Solve.

3. 10 × 100,000 = _____

4. 2,000 ÷ 100 = _____

Write the value of the underlined digit.

5. <u>2</u>30,186 = _____

6. 34<u>3</u>,579 = _____

7. Write the number in standard form.

eleven thousand eight hundred forty-five

_____

8. Circle the standard form.

200,000 + 90,000 + 1,000 + 300 + 1

209,131   291,301   291,310

9. Write in word form.

245,006

_____

_____

10. Round 563,790 to each place value.

ten thousands _____

tens _____

hundreds _____

thousands _____

hundred thousands _____

Use **<**, **>**, or **=** to compare.

11. six thousand four hundred three  6,403

12. 60,800 ◯ 60,008

13. 820,030 ◯ 800,000 + 2,000 + 300

14. 1,000 + 70 ◯ 1,700

8   2   7   5

15. Build the largest whole number possible using the digits above. _____

16. Build the smallest whole number possible using the digits above. _____

17. Explain how you figured out the smallest number possible. _____

_____

Add or subtract.

18.   999
     + 999

19.   500
     − 437

20.   42,967
   − 7,165

21.   30,024
   + 6,358

Multiply.

22.   65
   × 11

23.   504
   ×   3

24.   29
   × 67

25. 1,824
   ×   9

Divide. Show the remainder if there is one.

26. $9\overline{)90}$

27. $4\overline{)576}$

28. $6\overline{)5,243}$

29. $7\overline{)8,513}$

Name _____ Date _____

Place Value

Circle the correct answer.

1. 8,000 is (10, 100, 1,000) times larger than 800.

2. 30,000 is (10, 100, 1,000) times larger than 300.

3. 10 is (10, 100, 1,000) times smaller than 1,000.

Solve.

4. 800 ÷ 80 = _____   **5.** 40 × 1,000 = _____

6. 5,000 ÷ 5 = _____   **7.** 60,000 ÷ 1,000 = _____

8. 1,000,000 ÷ 1,000 = _____   **9.** 500,000 ÷ 50,000 = _____

Write the value of the underlined digit.

10. 35,9_7_2 = _____   **11.** 183,9_8_4 = _____

12. _2_5,392 = _____   **13.** _4_73,927 = _____

14. _1_,000,000 = _____   **15.** 27,48_6_ = _____

Complete the chart.

	Standard Form	Word Form	Expanded Form
16.		five hundred thirty thousand six	
17.	24,850		
18.			500,000 + 40,000 + 9,000 + 200 + 40 + 2
19.	29,408		
20.			300,000 + 90,000 + 200 + 80 + 3

Rounding Numbers

Round to the nearest hundred.

1. 25,395 _____ **2.** 2,438 _____

3. 14,895 _____ **4.** 9,974 _____

5. 17,432 _____ **6.** 52,703 _____

Round to the nearest ten thousand.

7. 35,709 _____ **8.** 854,999 _____

9. 30,000 _____ **10.** 10,648 _____

11. 387,455 _____ **12.** 470,593 _____

Round the following number to each place value.

685,469

13. tens _____

14. hundreds _____

15. thousands _____

16. ten thousands _____

17. hundred thousands _____

18. When do you round a number up? _____

19. When do you round a number down? _____

20. Explain how you would round 437,875 to the nearest ten thousand. _____

_____

_____

_____

Use these cards to assess rounding numbers. Give a student the stack to sort by the highest place value: hundreds, thousands, etc. Or, for each card, have him round to a given place value. If a student is struggling with rounding numbers, assign one place value to round and have the student sort all of the cards into two piles: one where the digit would cause the number to be rounded up and one where the digit would cause the number to be rounded down. Then, have the student round each number to that place value. If desired, laminate the cards and allow students to use write-on/wipe-away markers to mark directly on the number to help with rounding.

35,750 **A**	495,597 **B**
9,037 **C**	973,284 **D**
95,702 **E**	384,999 **F**

12,320	849,621
G	H
26,389	384,001
I	J
937,354	904,904
K	L
750	37,433
M	N

Name _____ Date _____

Comparing Numbers

Use **<**, **>**, or **=** to compare.

1. 308 ◯ 830

2. 5 thousands ◯ 9 hundreds

3. 24,890 ◯ 25,123

4. 1,000,000 ◯ 999,999

5. three thousand ◯ three hundred thousand

6. 1,847 ◯ 18,470

7. 20,000 + 5,000 + 600 + 4 ◯ 25,604

8. four hundred twenty-three thousand ◯ 423

9. 70,000 + 7,000 + 500 + 80 ◯ 77,508

7   2   4   8

10. Build the largest whole number possible using the digits above. _____

11. Build the smallest whole number possible using the digits above. _____

12. Explain how you figured out the largest number possible. _____

_____

_____

Name _____ Date _____

Addition and Subtraction

Add or subtract.

1. 369
      + 925

2. 400
      − 148

3. 483
      + 468

4. 732
      + 269

5. 3,947
      + 8,482

6. 4,193
      − 2,837

7. 1,000
      − 389

8. 593
      − 299

9. 24,465
      +   34

10. 40,329
       −   77

11. 88,888
       + 22,222

12. 14,032
       + 93,832

13. 48,938
       − 37,295

14. 205,483
       − 34,930

15. 356,999
       + 395,385

16. 779,262
       − 671,258

17. 528,287
       + 471,713

18. 999,993
       −   5

19. 392,937
       − 364,570

20. 1,000,000
       −   24,399

Multiplication

Multiply.

1. $\begin{array}{r} 51 \\ \times\ 5 \\ \hline \end{array}$

2. $\begin{array}{r} 37 \\ \times\ 8 \\ \hline \end{array}$

3. $\begin{array}{r} 24 \\ \times\ 4 \\ \hline \end{array}$

4. $\begin{array}{r} 29 \\ \times\ 9 \\ \hline \end{array}$

5. $\begin{array}{r} 386 \\ \times\ \ \ 3 \\ \hline \end{array}$

6. $\begin{array}{r} 135 \\ \times\ \ \ 8 \\ \hline \end{array}$

7. $\begin{array}{r} 444 \\ \times\ \ \ 9 \\ \hline \end{array}$

8. $\begin{array}{r} 384 \\ \times\ \ \ 6 \\ \hline \end{array}$

9. $\begin{array}{r} 856 \\ \times\ \ \ 4 \\ \hline \end{array}$

10. $\begin{array}{r} 1,000 \\ \times\ \ \ \ \ \ 6 \\ \hline \end{array}$

11. $\begin{array}{r} 4,092 \\ \times\ \ \ \ \ \ 5 \\ \hline \end{array}$

12. $\begin{array}{r} 9,273 \\ \times\ \ \ \ \ \ 8 \\ \hline \end{array}$

13. $\begin{array}{r} 8,362 \\ \times\ \ \ \ \ \ 6 \\ \hline \end{array}$

14. $\begin{array}{r} 2,706 \\ \times\ \ \ \ \ \ 7 \\ \hline \end{array}$

15. $\begin{array}{r} 3,075 \\ \times\ \ \ \ \ \ 9 \\ \hline \end{array}$

Multiplication

Multiply.

1. 83
   × 38

2. 47
   × 27

3. 31
   × 20

4. 52
   × 48

5. 96
   × 93

6. 83
   × 54

7. 12
   × 12

8. 20
   × 40

9. 82
   × 19

10. 47
    × 36

11. 55
    × 18

12. 72
    × 39

13. 46
    × 30

14. 11
    × 11

15. 99
    × 99

Division

Divide.

1. $7\overline{)35}$

2. $8\overline{)24}$

3. $3\overline{)48}$

4. $6\overline{)78}$

5. $9\overline{)144}$

6. $2\overline{)120}$

7. $4\overline{)160}$

8. $6\overline{)150}$

Divide. Show the remainder.

9. $3\overline{)28}$

10. $9\overline{)40}$

11. $5\overline{)64}$

12. $4\overline{)31}$

13. $6\overline{)25}$

14. $3\overline{)31}$

Division

Divide. Show the remainder if there is one.

1. 5)342

2. 3)291

3. 4)8,925

4. 3)405

5. 5)2,732

6. 3)1,011

7. 7)365

8. 2)123

9. 8)5,604

10. 4)6,251

11. 3)2,447

12. 9)4,896

A

Circle the correct answer.

4,000 is (10, 100, 1,000) times larger than 400.

4 is (10, 100, 1,000) times smaller than 400.

B

Solve.

6,000 ÷ 600 = _____

6,000 ÷ 10 = _____

C

Circle the number in the hundreds place.

452,630

Circle the number in the hundred thousands place.

908,127

Circle the number in the ten thousands place.

734,980

D

Write each number in standard form.

700,000 + 4,000 + 500 + 60 + 2

_____

twenty-five thousand nine hundred

_____

_____

E

Write 483,984 in expanded form.

F

Circle the standard form for **three hundred nine thousand eight**.

309,008   398,000

398   398,008

G

Write 345,275 in word form.

_____

_____

_____

_____

_____

H

Round each number to the nearest hundred.

853 _____

3,948 _____

12,038 _____

45,999 _____

Round 948,095 to each place value.

ten thousands _____

thousands _____

hundred thousands _____

tens _____

I

Use **<**, **>**, or **=** to compare.

800,000 ◯ 788,999

462,000 ◯ 400,000 + 60,000 + 200

four hundred nine ◯ four hundred ninety

J

Add.

$$3,475$$
$$+ 2,287$$

$$9,959$$
$$+ 9,959$$

K

Subtract.

$$6,452$$
$$- 3,570$$

$$1,000$$
$$- 686$$

L

Multiply.

$$498$$
$$\times\ \ \ 8$$

$$5,406$$
$$\times\ \ \ 7$$

M

Multiply.

$$43$$
$$\times 58$$

$$26$$
$$\times 63$$

N

Divide.

$3\overline{)93}$ $8\overline{)120}$

O

Divide. Show the remainder.

$4\overline{)93}$ $9\overline{)345}$ $6\overline{)3,205}$

P

Show What You Know
Number and Operations—Fractions

Complete the equivalent fractions.

1. $\dfrac{1}{2} = \dfrac{3}{}$

2. $\dfrac{1}{6} = \dfrac{}{12}$

Create an equivalent fraction.

3. $\dfrac{3}{5} = \text{—}$

4. $\dfrac{5}{6} = \text{—}$

Rewrite each fraction pair with common denominators.

5. $\dfrac{1}{2} \rightarrow \text{—}$

$\dfrac{2}{3} \rightarrow \text{—}$

6. $\dfrac{1}{4} \rightarrow \text{—}$

$\dfrac{1}{3} \rightarrow \text{—}$

Use **<**, **>**, or **=** to compare.

7. $\dfrac{1}{2} \bigcirc \dfrac{5}{10}$

8. $\dfrac{1}{4} \bigcirc \dfrac{3}{8}$

9. $\dfrac{3}{12} \bigcirc \dfrac{1}{6}$

10. $\dfrac{1}{8} \bigcirc \dfrac{3}{16}$

Add or subtract.

11. $\dfrac{1}{3} + \dfrac{1}{3} =$

12. $\dfrac{5}{12} + \dfrac{1}{12} =$

13. $\dfrac{5}{6} - \dfrac{1}{6} =$

14. $\dfrac{38}{100} + \dfrac{46}{100} =$

Complete the fractions to make each statement true.

15. $\dfrac{3}{4} = \dfrac{1}{4} + \dfrac{}{\text{—}} + \dfrac{}{\text{—}}$

16. $\dfrac{}{6} = \dfrac{1}{6} + \dfrac{1}{6} + \dfrac{1}{6}$

17. $\dfrac{5}{6} = \dfrac{1}{6} + \dfrac{4}{}$

18. $\dfrac{3}{8} = \dfrac{1}{8} + \dfrac{}{8}$

Add or subtract.

19. $4\dfrac{1}{3} + \dfrac{1}{3} =$ _____

20. $12\dfrac{1}{12} + 4\dfrac{7}{12} =$ _____

21. $8\dfrac{3}{4} - \dfrac{3}{4} =$ _____

22. $14\dfrac{2}{6} - 4\dfrac{1}{6} =$ _____

Solve.

23. A recipe calls for $\frac{1}{4}$ teaspoon salt and $\frac{2}{4}$ teaspoon baking soda. How much salt and baking soda does the recipe need?

_____

24. In jar of marbles, $\frac{1}{6}$ are blue and $\frac{4}{6}$ are yellow. What fraction of the marbles are not blue or yellow?

_____

Fill in the missing numbers.

If $\frac{7}{8} = 7 \times \left(\frac{1}{8} \right)$, then

25. $\frac{4}{5} = \boxed{} \times \left(\frac{}{} \right)$

26. $\frac{3}{10} = \boxed{} \times \left(\frac{}{} \right)$

Multiply.

27. $6 \times \frac{1}{2} = $ _____   **28.** $7 \times \frac{7}{10} = $ _____

Solve.

29. A craft requires $\frac{1}{4}$ of a sheet of paper. If 3 children are making the craft, how much paper is needed? _____

30. Some friends are making desserts for the school bake sale. Each child needs $\frac{1}{2}$ bag of marshmallows. If there are 6 children, how many bags of marshmallows do they need? _____

31. $\frac{4}{10} = \frac{}{100}$ $\frac{6}{10} = \frac{}{100}$

32. If $\frac{6}{10} = 0.6$, then $\frac{3}{10} = $ _____ .

Locate the answer on the number line.

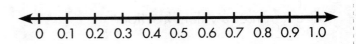

33. If the fraction $\frac{32}{100} = 0.32$, then $\frac{58}{100} = $ _____ .

Locate the answer on the number line.

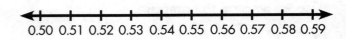

Find the decimal equivalent for each fraction.

34. $\frac{3}{10} = $ _____   **35.** $\frac{51}{100} = $ _____

Use **<**, **>**, or **=** to compare.

36. 0.3 $\bigcirc$ 0.6   **37.** 0.2 $\bigcirc$ 0.4

38. 0.73 $\bigcirc$ 0.78   **39.** 0.45 $\bigcirc$ 0.44

Name _____   Date _____

Show What You Know
Number and Operations—Fractions

Complete the equivalent fractions.

1. $\dfrac{1}{5} = \dfrac{2}{}$

2. $\dfrac{3}{10} = \dfrac{}{100}$

Create an equivalent fraction.

3. $\dfrac{1}{4} = \rule{2em}{0.4pt}$

4. $\dfrac{5}{8} = \rule{2em}{0.4pt}$

Rewrite each fraction pair with common denominators.

5. $\dfrac{1}{4} \rightarrow \rule{2em}{0.4pt}$

$\dfrac{1}{6} \rightarrow \rule{2em}{0.4pt}$

6. $\dfrac{1}{5} \rightarrow \rule{2em}{0.4pt}$

$\dfrac{2}{3} \rightarrow \rule{2em}{0.4pt}$

Use **<**, **>**, or **=** to compare.

7. $\dfrac{1}{4} \bigcirc \dfrac{1}{8}$

8. $\dfrac{1}{5} \bigcirc \dfrac{5}{10}$

9. $\dfrac{4}{12} \bigcirc \dfrac{1}{4}$

10. $\dfrac{3}{10} \bigcirc \dfrac{3}{20}$

Add or subtract.

11. $\dfrac{3}{8} + \dfrac{3}{8} =$

12. $\dfrac{26}{100} + \dfrac{9}{100} =$

13. $\dfrac{7}{12} - \dfrac{1}{12} =$

14. $\dfrac{8}{10} - \dfrac{3}{10} =$

Complete the fractions to make each statement true.

15. $\rule{2em}{0.4pt} = \dfrac{1}{8} + \dfrac{1}{8} + \dfrac{1}{8} + \dfrac{1}{8}$

16. $\dfrac{}{10} = \dfrac{5}{10} + \dfrac{4}{10}$

17. $\dfrac{5}{8} = \dfrac{}{} + \dfrac{1}{8}$

18. $\dfrac{4}{6} = \dfrac{2}{6} + \dfrac{}{6} + \dfrac{1}{6}$

Add or subtract.

19. $8\dfrac{3}{10} + 2\dfrac{1}{10} = \rule{4em}{0.4pt}$

20. $9\dfrac{5}{8} + 9\dfrac{2}{8} = \rule{4em}{0.4pt}$

21. $10\dfrac{3}{8} - 2\dfrac{1}{8} = \rule{4em}{0.4pt}$

22. $23\dfrac{4}{5} - \dfrac{1}{5} = \rule{4em}{0.4pt}$

Solve.

23. Marc planned to run $\frac{3}{4}$ of a mile. He has already run $\frac{1}{4}$ of a mile. How much more does he have left to run?

_____

24. In Oak Park, $\frac{2}{8}$ of the trees around the school are maples. Of the total, $\frac{4}{8}$ are oaks. How many trees are maples and oaks?

_____

Fill in the missing numbers.

If $\frac{6}{10} = 6 \times \left(\frac{1}{10} \right)$, then

25. $\frac{2}{5} = \boxed{} \times \left(\text{—} \right)$

26. $\frac{7}{12} = \boxed{} \times \left(\text{—} \right)$

Multiply.

27. $6 \times \frac{2}{5} =$ _____   **28.** $3 \times \frac{7}{12} =$ _____

Solve.

29. A group is creating birdhouses. Each person needs $\frac{1}{8}$ of a wooden dowel. If there are 7 people, will they need 1 or 2 dowels? _____

30. An animal rescue gives each dog $\frac{3}{4}$ cups of dog food for breakfast. If there are 5 dogs, how many cups of dog food are needed? _____

31. $\frac{1}{10} = \frac{}{100}$ $\frac{2}{10} = \frac{}{100}$

32. $\frac{9}{10} + \frac{20}{100}$

33. If $\frac{8}{10} = 0.8$, then $\frac{2}{10} =$ _____ .

Locate the answer on the number line.

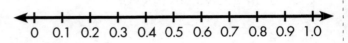

34. If the fraction $\frac{44}{100} = 0.44$, then $\frac{53}{100} =$ _____ .

Locate the answer on the number line.

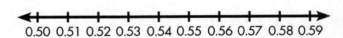

Find the decimal equivalent for each fraction.

35. $\frac{8}{10} =$ _____   **36.** $\frac{57}{100} =$ _____

Use **<**, **>**, or **=** to compare.

37. 0.2 $\bigcirc$ 0.8   **38.** 1 $\bigcirc$ 0.7

39. 0.85 $\bigcirc$ 0.58   **40.** 0.02 $\bigcirc$ 0.02

Name _____ Date _____

Equivalent Fractions

Complete the models to show equivalent fractions.

1. $\frac{1}{2} = \frac{2}{4}$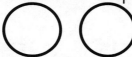

2. $\frac{1}{3} = \frac{3}{9}$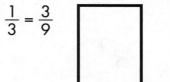

Complete each fraction to make a true statement.

3. If $\frac{1}{2} = \frac{2}{4}$ then $\frac{1}{6} = \frac{2}{\_\_\_}$.

4. If $\frac{3}{4} = \frac{9}{12}$ then $\frac{4}{5} = \frac{\_\_\_}{15}$.

5. If $\frac{2}{3} = \frac{10}{15}$ then $\frac{5}{6} = \frac{\_\_\_}{30}$.

Complete each fraction to make equivalent fractions.

6. $\frac{4}{5} = \frac{12}{\_\_\_}$

7. $\frac{7}{8} = \frac{14}{\_\_\_}$

8. $\frac{3}{8} = \frac{\_\_\_}{56}$

9. $\frac{4}{12} = \frac{\_\_\_}{36}$

Create an equivalent fraction. Then, explain how you created the equivalent fraction.

10. $\frac{4}{5} = \text{—}$

_____

11. $\frac{5}{7} = \text{—}$

_____

12. $\frac{3}{10} = \text{—}$

_____

Create three equivalent fractions for each fraction.

13. $\frac{1}{2}$ —, —, —

14. $\frac{1}{4}$ —, —, —

15. $\frac{1}{5}$ —, —, —

16. $\frac{3}{8}$ —, —, —

17. Explain how to create a fraction equivalent to $\frac{4}{5}$. _____

_____

Comparing Fractions

Label each fraction. Then, use **<**, **>**, or **=** to compare.

1.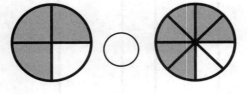

_____   _____

2. 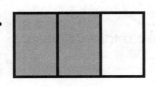 ◯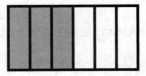

_____   _____

3.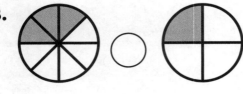

_____   _____

4.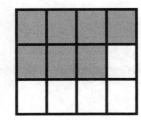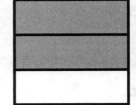

_____   _____

Complete the fraction models. Then, use **<**, **>**, or **=** to compare.

5. $\frac{3}{4}$ ◯ $\frac{1}{2}$ ◯ ◯

6. $\frac{4}{5}$ ◯ $\frac{8}{10}$ ▭ ▭

7. $\frac{2}{3}$ ◯ $\frac{3}{4}$ ◯ ◯

8. $\frac{1}{8}$ ◯ $\frac{1}{6}$ ▭ ▭

Use **<**, **>**, or **=** to compare.

9. $\frac{1}{3}$ ◯ $\frac{1}{4}$

10. $\frac{1}{4}$ ◯ $\frac{3}{12}$

11. $\frac{2}{5}$ ◯ $\frac{3}{10}$

12. $\frac{50}{100}$ ◯ $\frac{8}{10}$

Comparing Fractions

Use these cards to assess students' understanding of comparing fractions and equivalent fractions. Have a student sort cards by whether they are greater than or less than $\frac{1}{2}$. Or, flip over two cards and have her identify which fraction is greater (or whether they are equivalent). Finally, you may choose to have her match equivalent fractions.

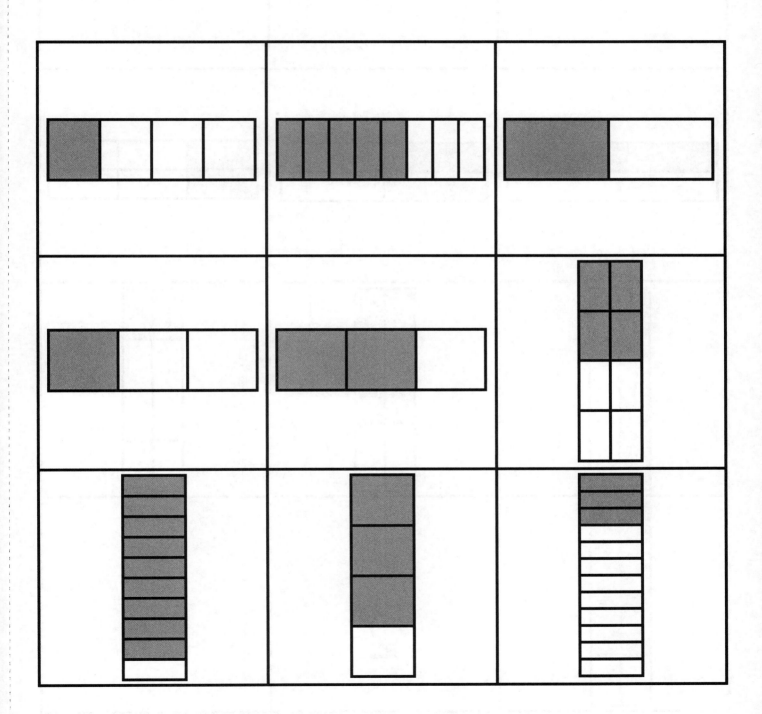

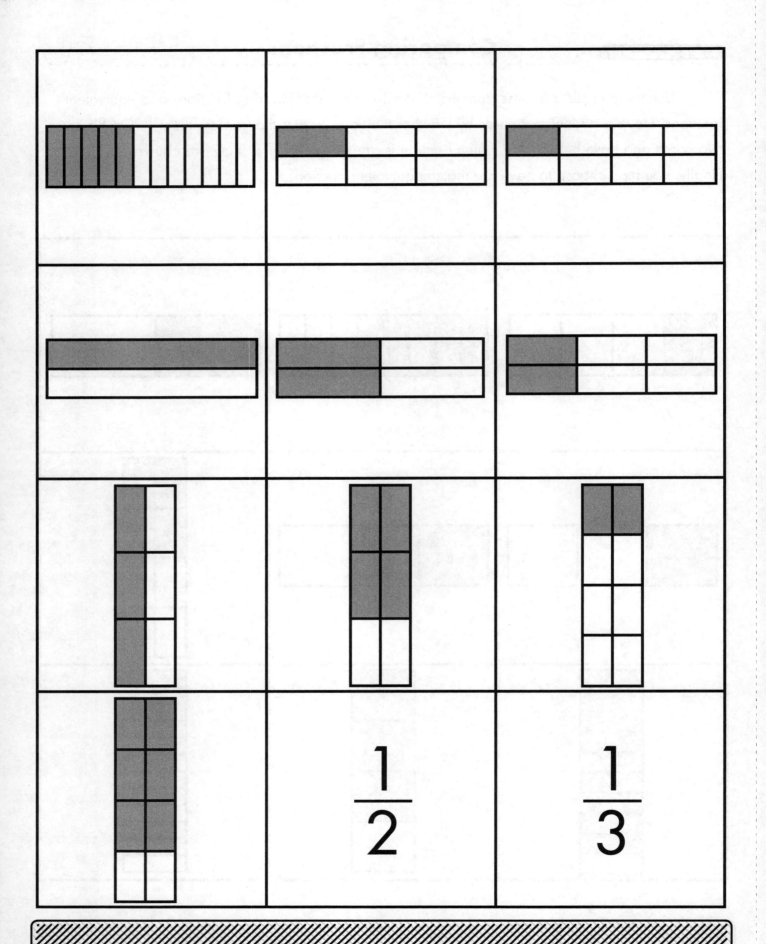

$\dfrac{2}{3}$	$\dfrac{1}{4}$	$\dfrac{2}{4}$
$\dfrac{3}{4}$	$\dfrac{1}{6}$	$\dfrac{2}{6}$
$\dfrac{3}{6}$	$\dfrac{4}{6}$	$\dfrac{1}{8}$
$\dfrac{2}{8}$	$\dfrac{4}{8}$	$\dfrac{6}{8}$

Finding Common Denominators

1. Draw an **X** over each fraction pair that is not equivalent.

$\frac{1}{2} = \frac{3}{6}$ $\qquad\qquad$ $\frac{1}{4} = \frac{4}{8}$ $\qquad\qquad$ $\frac{3}{4} = \frac{4}{12}$ $\qquad\qquad$ $\frac{1}{5} = \frac{2}{20}$

2. Choose one of the fractions that you crossed out in problem 1. Draw and label a model to show why they were not equivalent.

Rewrite each fraction pair with common denominators.

3. $\frac{1}{2} \rightarrow$ __

$\frac{3}{4} \rightarrow$ __

4. $\frac{2}{3} \rightarrow$ __

$\frac{1}{4} \rightarrow$ __

5. $\frac{1}{3} \rightarrow$ __

$\frac{2}{6} \rightarrow$ __

6. $\frac{2}{10} \rightarrow$ __

$\frac{3}{5} \rightarrow$ __

7. $\frac{1}{2} \rightarrow$ __

$\frac{3}{5} \rightarrow$ __

8. $\frac{1}{2} \rightarrow$ __

$\frac{2}{3} \rightarrow$ __

Use common denominators to compare each set of fractions. Then, use **<**, **>**, or **=** to compare.

9. $\frac{1}{2} \bigcirc \frac{3}{10}$

10. $\frac{1}{4} \bigcirc \frac{2}{8}$

11. $\frac{3}{12} \bigcirc \frac{1}{3}$

12. $\frac{1}{6} \bigcirc \frac{3}{12}$

Adding Fractions

Add.

1. $\dfrac{1}{5} + \dfrac{3}{5} =$

2. $\dfrac{5}{8} + \dfrac{1}{8} =$

3. $\dfrac{3}{10} + \dfrac{4}{10} =$

4. $\dfrac{1}{4} + \dfrac{3}{4} =$

5. $\dfrac{1}{6} + \dfrac{2}{6} =$

6. $\dfrac{2}{8} + \dfrac{5}{8} =$

7. $\dfrac{7}{10} + \dfrac{7}{10} =$

8. $\dfrac{4}{12} + \dfrac{5}{12} =$

9. $\dfrac{11}{12} + \dfrac{11}{12} =$

10. $\dfrac{28}{100} + \dfrac{82}{100} =$

11. $\dfrac{35}{100} + \dfrac{24}{100} =$

12. $\dfrac{47}{100} + \dfrac{29}{100} =$

13. $\dfrac{1}{3} + \dfrac{2}{3} + \dfrac{1}{3} =$

14. $\dfrac{2}{8} + \dfrac{1}{8} + \dfrac{3}{8} =$

15. $\dfrac{9}{10} + \dfrac{1}{10} + \dfrac{4}{10} =$

16. $\dfrac{7}{12} + \dfrac{3}{12} + \dfrac{4}{12} =$

17. $\dfrac{2}{100} + \dfrac{57}{100} + \dfrac{28}{100} =$

18. $\dfrac{3}{100} + \dfrac{34}{100} + \dfrac{20}{100} =$

Subtracting Fractions

Subtract.

1. $\dfrac{5}{8} - \dfrac{1}{8} =$

2. $\dfrac{3}{4} - \dfrac{1}{4} =$

3. $\dfrac{5}{6} - \dfrac{3}{6} =$

4. $\dfrac{9}{10} - \dfrac{9}{10} =$

5. $\dfrac{8}{8} - \dfrac{1}{8} =$

6. $\dfrac{12}{12} - \dfrac{6}{12} =$

7. $\dfrac{11}{12} - \dfrac{7}{12} =$

8. $\dfrac{56}{100} - \dfrac{14}{100} =$

9. $\dfrac{11}{12} - \dfrac{1}{12} =$

10. $\dfrac{93}{100} - \dfrac{55}{100} =$

11. $\dfrac{6}{12} - \dfrac{5}{12} =$

12. $\dfrac{99}{100} - \dfrac{49}{100} =$

13. $\dfrac{73}{100} - \dfrac{28}{100} =$

14. $\dfrac{7}{8} - \dfrac{1}{8} - \dfrac{1}{8} =$

15. $\dfrac{11}{12} - \dfrac{4}{12} - \dfrac{6}{12} =$

16. $\dfrac{83}{100} - \dfrac{40}{100} - \dfrac{3}{100} =$

Decomposing Fractions

Decompose each fraction.

1. $\dfrac{2}{4} = \dfrac{1}{4} + \underline{}$

2. $\dfrac{3}{6} = \dfrac{1}{6} + \underline{} + \underline{}$

3. $\dfrac{}{5} = \dfrac{1}{5} + \dfrac{1}{5}$

4. $\dfrac{}{8} = \dfrac{1}{8} + \dfrac{1}{8} + \dfrac{1}{8} + \dfrac{1}{8}$

5. $\underline{} = \dfrac{1}{10} + \dfrac{1}{10} + \dfrac{1}{10} + \dfrac{1}{10} + \dfrac{1}{10}$

Complete the fractions to make each statement true.

6. $\dfrac{3}{4} = \dfrac{1}{4} + \dfrac{2}{}$ **7.** $\dfrac{5}{8} = \dfrac{1}{8} + \dfrac{}{8}$

8. $\dfrac{}{12} = \dfrac{6}{12} + \dfrac{5}{12}$ **9.** $\dfrac{5}{6} = \dfrac{}{6} + \dfrac{3}{6}$

10. Decompose $\dfrac{6}{10}$ in two ways.

$\dfrac{1}{10} + \dfrac{}{10} = \dfrac{6}{10}$ $\dfrac{4}{10} + \dfrac{}{10} = \dfrac{6}{10}$

11. Decompose $\dfrac{5}{12}$ in two ways.

$\dfrac{4}{12} + \dfrac{}{12} = \dfrac{5}{12}$ $\dfrac{3}{12} + \dfrac{}{12} = \dfrac{5}{12}$

12. Decompose $\dfrac{21}{100}$ in two ways.

$\dfrac{}{100} + \dfrac{}{100} = \dfrac{21}{100}$ $\dfrac{}{100} + \dfrac{}{100} = \dfrac{21}{100}$

13. Decompose $\dfrac{8}{11}$ in two ways.

$\underline{} + \underline{} = \dfrac{8}{11}$ $\underline{} + \underline{} = \dfrac{8}{11}$

14. Decompose $\dfrac{13}{18}$ in two ways.

$\underline{} + \underline{} = \dfrac{13}{18}$ $\underline{} + \underline{} = \dfrac{13}{18}$

15. Decompose $\dfrac{11}{12}$ in two ways.

$\dfrac{11}{12} = $ _____

$\dfrac{11}{12} = $ _____

16. Decompose $\dfrac{60}{100}$ in two ways.

$\dfrac{60}{100} = $ _____

$\dfrac{60}{100} = $ _____

Name _____ Date _____

Operations with Mixed Numbers

Solve by drawing a fraction model.

1. $3\dfrac{1}{3} + 2\dfrac{1}{3} =$ _____

2. $2\dfrac{1}{4} + 1\dfrac{1}{4} =$ _____

Add.

3. $6\dfrac{1}{4} + \dfrac{1}{4} =$ _____

4. $7\dfrac{3}{8} + 3\dfrac{3}{8} =$ _____

5. $8\dfrac{1}{10} + 7\dfrac{7}{10} =$ _____

6. $4\dfrac{1}{5} + 9\dfrac{2}{5} =$ _____

7. $5\dfrac{5}{12} + 9\dfrac{7}{12} =$ _____

8. $48\dfrac{47}{100} + 31\dfrac{19}{100} =$ _____

Subtract.

9. $4\dfrac{3}{4} - \dfrac{1}{4} =$ _____

10. $7\dfrac{4}{6} - 5\dfrac{2}{6} =$ _____

11. $10\dfrac{9}{10} - 4\dfrac{1}{10} =$ _____

12. $84\dfrac{5}{8} - 19\dfrac{3}{8} =$ _____

13. $8\dfrac{11}{12} - \dfrac{7}{12} =$ _____

14. $67\dfrac{93}{100} - 49\dfrac{26}{100} =$ _____

Name _____ Date _____

Fraction Word Problems

Solve by drawing a fraction model.

1. John ate $\frac{1}{5}$ of a pizza. His dad ate $\frac{3}{5}$ of a pizza. How much of the pizza did they eat? _____

Write the related equation. Then, solve.

2. Taylor spent $\frac{1}{4}$ of an hour doing her homework. She spent another $\frac{1}{4}$ of an hour eating a snack. What fraction of an hour remains?

Write the equation. _____

3. A recipe calls for $\frac{1}{4}$ cup of white sugar and $\frac{1}{4}$ cup of brown sugar. How much sugar is used in all?

Write the equation. _____

4. On the checkerboard, $\frac{4}{10}$ of the pieces left are red. What fraction of the pieces left are black?

Write the equation. _____

5. A fish tank contains an assortment of fish. Of the fish, $\frac{6}{10}$ are yellow, $\frac{1}{10}$ are blue, and $\frac{2}{10}$ are orange. How many fish are yellow, blue, or orange?

Write the equation. _____

How many fish are not yellow, blue, or orange? _____

Name _____   Date _____

Multiplying Fractions

Fill in the missing numbers.

If $\dfrac{5}{6} = 5 \times \left(\dfrac{1}{6}\right)$, then

1. $\dfrac{3}{8} = \boxed{} \times \left(\dfrac{}{}\right)$

2. $\dfrac{2}{5} = \boxed{} \times \left(\dfrac{}{}\right)$

3. $\dfrac{4}{10} = \boxed{} \times \left(\dfrac{}{}\right)$

4. $\dfrac{35}{100} = \boxed{} \times \left(\dfrac{}{}\right)$

Multiply. Change improper fractions to mixed numbers.

5. $6 \times \dfrac{1}{6} = $ _____

6. $2 \times \dfrac{1}{8} = $ _____

7. $8 \times \dfrac{5}{12} = $ _____

8. $10 \times \dfrac{3}{10} = $ _____

9. $3 \times \dfrac{2}{3} = $ _____

10. $6 \times \dfrac{3}{4} = $ _____

11. $5 \times \dfrac{40}{100} = $ _____

12. $4 \times \dfrac{2}{5} = $ _____

Solve. Write the equation you used.

13. There are 5 kids at a party. They will each get $\dfrac{1}{4}$ of a pizza. How many pizzas should they

order? _____

Equation: _____

14. The members of the track team are each running $\dfrac{1}{5}$ of a mile. If there are 6 members on the

team, will they have run more than 1 mile all together? _____

How much will they have run in all? _____

Equation: _____

15. Each student in each group needs $\dfrac{3}{4}$ cup of colored water for an experiment. There are

4 students in a group. How many cups of water will each group need? _____

Equation: _____

Fractions and Decimals

Complete each fraction to make the statement true.

1. If $\frac{3}{10} = \frac{30}{100}$, then $\frac{7}{10} = \frac{}{100}$.

2. If $\frac{9}{10} = \frac{90}{100}$, then $\frac{2}{10} = \frac{}{100}$.

3. If $\frac{4}{10} = \frac{40}{100}$, then $\frac{5}{10} = \frac{}{100}$.

Complete each statement. Then, locate the answer on the number line.

4. If $\frac{9}{10} = 0.9$, then $\frac{2}{10} = $ _____ .

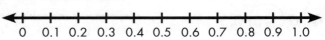

5. If $\frac{1}{10} = 0.1$, then $\frac{6}{10} = $ _____ .

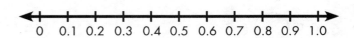

6. If $\frac{45}{100} = 0.45$, then $\frac{78}{100} = $ _____ .

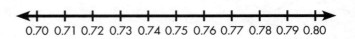

7. If $\frac{19}{100} = 0.19$, then $\frac{22}{100} = $ _____ .

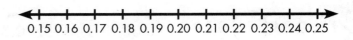

8. If $\frac{99}{100} = 0.99$, then $\frac{34}{100} = $ _____ .

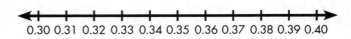

Write the decimal equivalent for each fraction.

9. $\frac{4}{10} = $ _____

10. $\frac{7}{10} = $ _____

11. $\frac{58}{100} = $ _____

12. $\frac{2}{100} = $ _____

Add.

13. $\frac{6}{10} + \frac{5}{100} = $ _____

14. $\frac{1}{10} + \frac{10}{100} = $ _____

15. $\frac{5}{10} + \frac{18}{100} = $ _____

Comparing Decimals

Place each number on the number line. Then, use **<**, **>**, or **=** to compare.

1. 0.4 ◯ 0.9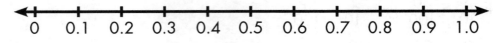

2. 0.5 ◯ 0.1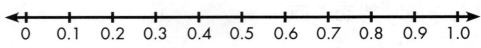

3. 0.1 ◯ 1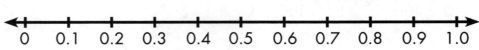

4. 0 ◯ 0.5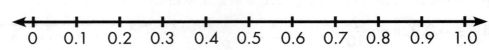

Use **<**, **>**, or **=** to compare.

5. 0.9 ◯ 0.3   **6.** 1 ◯ 0.4

7. 0.9 ◯ 0.6   **8.** 0.1 ◯ 0.9

9 0.4 ◯ 1   **10.** 0.3 ◯ 0.1

Place each number on the number line. Then, use **<**, **>**, or **=** to compare.

11. 0.34 ◯ 0.39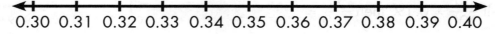

12. 0.08 ◯ 0.03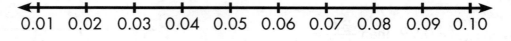

13. 0.48 ◯ 0.52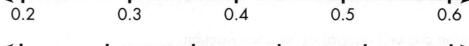

14. 0.38 ◯ 0.02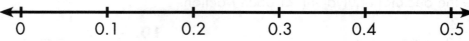

Use **<**, **>**, or **=** to compare.

15. 0.27 ◯ 0.28   **16.** 0.89 ◯ 0.82

17. 0.03 ◯ 0.09   **18.** 0.41 ◯ 0.14

19. 0.01 ◯ 0.10   **20.** 0.47 ◯ 1

Use the following cards to assess students' ability to compare decimals. First, turn over two cards. Have a student point to the larger decimal. If a student is struggling, have him sort the cards by whether the decimals show only the tenths or include the hundredths place value. Then, work with only the cards in the tenths place value. The cards can also be used to have students order a set of decimals from lowest to highest. If desired, laminate the cards and allow students to use write-on/wipe-away markers.

0	0.1	0.2
0.3	0.4	0.5
0.6	0.7	0.8

0.9	0.45	0.48
0.29	0.02	0.20
0.52	0.59	0.10
0.97	0.18	0.33

A. Complete the fractions to make each pair equivalent.

$$\frac{3}{5} = \frac{}{10} \qquad \frac{1}{6} = \frac{2}{}$$

B. Draw an **X** over each fraction pair that is not equivalent.

$$\frac{1}{2} = \frac{4}{8} \qquad\qquad \frac{1}{4} = \frac{4}{12}$$

$$\frac{1}{6} = \frac{2}{3} \qquad\qquad \frac{1}{3} = \frac{2}{6}$$

C. Rewrite each fraction pair with common denominators.

$$\frac{1}{2} \rightarrow \underline{\quad} \qquad \frac{3}{10} \rightarrow \underline{\quad}$$

$$\frac{3}{4} \rightarrow \underline{\quad} \qquad \frac{71}{100} \rightarrow \underline{\quad}$$

D. Use **<**, **>**, or **=** to compare.

$$\frac{1}{2} \bigcirc \frac{4}{12} \qquad\qquad \frac{2}{3} \bigcirc \frac{4}{12}$$

$$\frac{1}{5} \bigcirc \frac{3}{10} \qquad\qquad \frac{5}{8} \bigcirc \frac{3}{4}$$

E. Add.

$$\frac{1}{6} + \frac{3}{6} = \qquad \frac{1}{10} + \frac{7}{10} =$$

$$\frac{1}{10} + \frac{3}{10} = \qquad \frac{37}{100} + \frac{22}{100} =$$

F. Subtract.

$$\frac{4}{5} - \frac{4}{5} = \qquad \frac{1}{2} - \frac{1}{2} =$$

$$\frac{5}{8} - \frac{1}{8} = \qquad \frac{64}{100} - \frac{48}{100} =$$

G. Decompose each fraction.

$$\frac{3}{8} = \frac{1}{8} + \underline{\quad} + \underline{\quad}$$

$$\frac{}{12} = \frac{1}{12} + \frac{1}{12} + \frac{1}{12}$$

$$\frac{7}{8} = \frac{2}{8} + \frac{5}{}$$

$$\frac{9}{10} = \frac{4}{10} + \frac{}{10}$$

H. Add.

$$7\frac{1}{5} + 1\frac{1}{5} = \underline{\qquad\qquad}$$

$$4\frac{2}{10} + 9\frac{3}{10} = \underline{\qquad\qquad}$$

$$7\frac{26}{100} + 8\frac{9}{100} = \underline{\qquad\qquad}$$

Subtract.

$$14\frac{3}{4} - 14\frac{3}{4} = \underline{\hspace{2cm}}$$

$$4\frac{3}{4} - 2\frac{1}{4} = \underline{\hspace{2cm}}$$

$$3\frac{5}{6} - 3\frac{4}{6} = \underline{\hspace{2cm}}$$

I

Solve.

Elizabeth ran $\frac{3}{4}$ of a mile. Her sister Aubrie ran $\frac{1}{4}$ of a mile. How much farther did Elizabeth run than Aubrie? \underline{\hspace{2cm}}

A recipe calls for $\frac{1}{4}$ cup oats and $\frac{2}{4}$ cup milk. How much oats and milk are used in the recipe in all? \underline{\hspace{2cm}}

J

Fill in the missing numbers.

If $\frac{5}{12} = 5 \times \left(\frac{1}{12}\right)$, then

$$\frac{6}{8} = \boxed{} \times \left(\frac{}{}\right) \qquad \boxed{} \times \left(\frac{}{}\right) = \frac{5}{12}$$

K

Solve.

The art club is creating sculptures. Each student needs $\frac{1}{8}$ cup of glue to make the sculpture. If there are 7 students, how much glue is needed?

\underline{\hspace{6cm}}

L

Fill in the missing number.

If $\frac{2}{10} = \frac{20}{100}$, then $\frac{9}{10} = \frac{}{100}$.

If $\frac{94}{100} = 0.94$, then $\frac{84}{100} = \underline{\hspace{2cm}}$.

Explain how you solved one of the problems.

\underline{\hspace{6cm}}

M

Write the equivalent decimal for each fraction.

$$\frac{8}{10} = \underline{\hspace{2cm}} \qquad \frac{1}{10} = \underline{\hspace{2cm}}$$

$$\frac{33}{100} = \underline{\hspace{2cm}} \qquad \frac{61}{100} = \underline{\hspace{2cm}}$$

N

Use <, >, or = to compare.

1. 0.6 $\bigcirc$ 0.2   **2.** 0.2 $\bigcirc$ 0.1

3. 0.1 $\bigcirc$ 0.3   **4.** 0.9 $\bigcirc$ 1

O

Use <, >, or = to compare.

1. 0.14 $\bigcirc$ 0.10   **2.** 0.07 $\bigcirc$ 0.01

3. 0.13 $\bigcirc$ 0.31   **4.** 0.91 $\bigcirc$ 0.09

P

Name _____ Date _____

✦ Show What You Know ✦
Measurement and Data

Circle the greatest amount in each set.

1.　8 milligrams　　　　8 kilograms　　　　8 grams

2.　1 centimeter　　　1 meter　　　　1 millimeter　　　1 kilometer

Solve.

3. 1 pound = _____ ounces, so 2 pounds = _____ ounces.

4. 1 hour = _____ minutes, so 4 hours = _____ minutes.

5. 1 dime = _____ nickels, so 5 dimes = _____ nickels.

Use **<**, **>**, or **=** to compare.

6.　900 milliliters ◯ 1 liter　　　　**7.** 8 meters ◯ 800 centimeters

Solve.

8. Sara is 58 inches tall. Her brother is 5 feet tall. Who is taller? _____

9. A bird weighs 1 pound, 11 ounces. How much does it weigh in ounces? _____

10. Mateo has $29. His brother, Santiago, has 3 times that much. How much money does

Santiago have? _____ How much do they have together? _____

Find the perimeter and area of each shape.

11.
```
      6 cm
 ┌──────────┐
 │          │ 3 cm
 └──────────┘
```
P = _____　A = _____

12.
```
        32 ft.
 ┌────────────────┐
 │                │ 8 ft.
 └────────────────┘
```
P = _____　A = _____

Solve.

13. A rectangular yard has a length of 24 meters and a width of 18 meters. How much fencing

would be needed to enclose the yard? _____

14. Connor is getting new carpeting in his bedroom. If his bedroom is 12 feet wide by 10 feet

long, how much carpeting does he need? _____

15. A rectangular picture frame has an area of 24 square inches. What are the possible

dimensions of the frame? _____

Use the line plot to answer the questions.

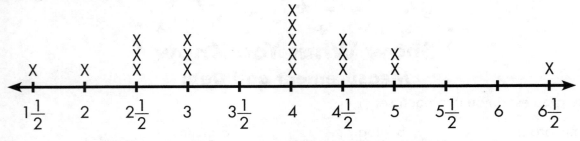

Height of Bean Plants in Mrs. Scott's Class (in.)

16. What is the difference in the height of the tallest and shortest plants? _____ in.

17. How many total plants are there? _____

Use a protractor to measure each angle.

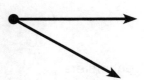

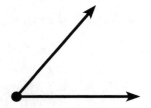

18. _____

19. _____

Complete each angle to match the measurement shown.

20. 120°

21. 70°

Find the measure of the missing angle.

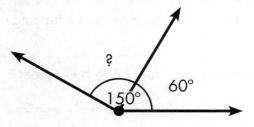

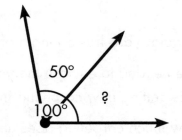

22. _____

23. _____

Name _____ Date _____

✦ Show What You Know ✦
Measurement and Data

Circle the greatest amount in each set.

1. 5 ounces   5 pounds

2. 1 kilogram   1 milligram   1 gram

Solve.

3. 1 dollar = _____ nickels, so 4 dollars = _____ nickels.

4. 1 meter = _____ centimeters, so 6 meters = _____ centimeters.

5. 1 pound = _____ ounces, so 10 pounds = _____ ounces.

Use **<**, **>**, or **=** to compare.

6. 65 ounces ( ) 4 pounds   **7.** 30 yards ( ) 100 feet

Solve.

8. Maggie's dog, Pepper, is 2 feet long. Her friend's dog, Luna, is 18 inches long. Which dog is longer? _____

9. McKenzie has 100 nickels. Alex has 500 pennies. Who has more money? _____

10. A race is 3 kilometers long. How many meters long is it? _____

Find the perimeter and area of the shapes.

11. 4 ft.
⬜ 4 ft.

P = _____   A = _____

12. 10 m
▭ 3 m

P = _____   A = _____

Solve.

13. A rectangular enclosure has a length of 90 centimeters and a width of 43 centimeters. How much fencing would be needed to go around all four sides of the enclosure? _____

14. A coffee table is 5 feet long by 4 feet wide. What is the area of the table? _____

15. A rectangular bulletin board has an area of 50 square feet. What are the possible dimensions of the bulletin board? _____

Use the line plot to answer the questions.

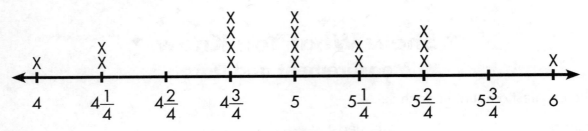

Heights of Students (ft.)

16. What is the difference in the height of the tallest and shortest students? _____ ft.

17. How many total students are there? _____

Use a protractor to measure each angle.

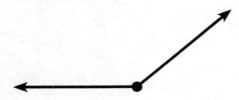

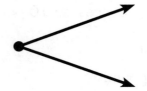

18. _____

19. _____

Complete each angle to match the measurement shown.

20. 20°

21. 150°

Find the measure of the missing angle.

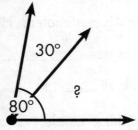

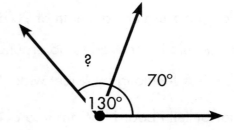

22. _____

23. _____

Measurement Word Problems

Solve. Show your work.

1. Katya is 42 inches tall. In order to ride The Spinner, you need to be 4 feet tall. Is she tall

enough? _____

2. A baby weighs 8 pounds, 1 ounce. How much does she weigh in ounces? _____

3. A sub sandwich is 3 feet long. How many inches long is it? _____

4. An ant traveled 4 inches. What fraction of a foot did it travel? _____

5. A bottle contains 2 liters of juice. How many milliliters of juice is that? _____

6. Tara's baby brother has been napping for $1\frac{1}{2}$ hours. How many minutes has he been

napping? _____

7. Shane has run 4 kilometers. How many meters has he run? _____

Solve.

8. A bag of apples weighs $2\frac{3}{4}$ pounds. A bunch of bananas weighs $1\frac{1}{4}$ pound. How much more do the apples weigh than the bananas? _____

How much does all of the fruit weigh together? _____

9. What fraction of a dollar is…

a quarter? _____   a dime? _____

a nickel? _____   a penny? _____

10. A stick of celery is 13 inches long. If it needs to be divided equally between 4 children, what length piece will each child get? _____

How much is left over? _____

11. Mr. Thompson's class has been growing plants for 3 weeks. How many days have they been growing plants? _____

12. Blake is 49 inches tall. Is he over 3 feet tall? _____

Is he over 4 feet tall? _____

13. Olivia has $39. Her sister, Sophia, has 4 times that much. How much money does Sophia have? _____

How much money do they have together? _____

How much more money does Sophia have than Olivia? _____

14. A male gorilla named Bruce weighs 200 kilograms. A female gorilla named Bonnie weighs 168,000 grams. Which gorilla weighs more? _____

Explain. _____

_____

Name _____ Date _____

Units of Measure

Circle the greater amount.

1. 1 liter   1 milliliter   **2.** 2 centimeters   2 meters

3. 5 inches   5 feet   **4.** 20 kilograms   20 grams

5. 60 seconds   60 minutes   **6.** 1 pound   1 ounce

Write each set of units in order from smallest to largest.

7. centimeter   meter   millimeter   kilometer

_____

8. minutes   hours   seconds

_____

Complete the tables.

9.

cm	mm
1	
2	
3	
4	
5	

10.

ft.	in.
1	
2	
3	
4	
5	

Solve.

11. 2 pounds = _____ ounces   **12.** 3 hours = _____ minutes

13. 5 kilograms = _____ grams   **14.** 8 feet = _____ inches

15. 60 liters = _____ milliliters   **16.** 3 kilometers = _____ centimeters

Perimeter

Solve using the measurements given.

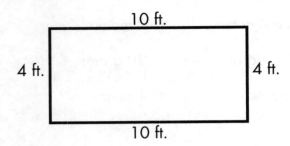

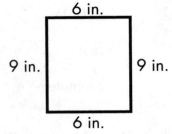

1. P = _____

2. P = _____

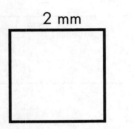

3. P = _____

4. P = _____

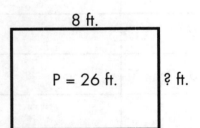

5. length = _____ ft.

6. width = _____ cm

7. Explain how to find the perimeter of a closed shape. _____

_____

8. Explain how you found the missing width in problem 6. _____

_____

9. Explain how you would find the perimeter of a square. _____

_____

Name _____ Date _____

Area

Solve using the measurements given.

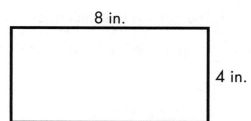

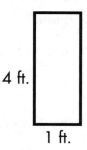

1. A = _____

2. A = _____

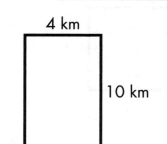

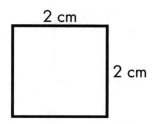

3. A = _____

4. A = _____

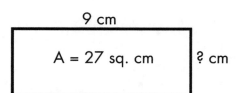

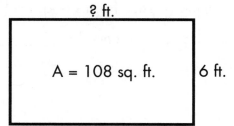

5. length = _____ cm

6. width = _____ ft.

7. Explain how you find the area of a closed shape. _____

_____

8. Explain how you found the missing number for number 6. _____

_____

9. Explain how finding the area of a square is different than finding the area of other rectangles.

_____

Area and Perimeter Word Problems

Solve. Then, circle the measurement you solved for.

1. A rectangular garden needs a fence to keep the rabbits out. The garden has dimensions of 99 centimeters long and 75 centimeters wide. How much fencing is needed for all four sides?

I found (perimeter, area) to solve the problem.

2. Cole and his sister, Mia, are getting carpeting in their bedrooms. Here are the sizes of their rooms.

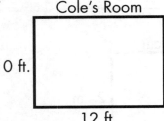

Cole's Room
10 ft.
12 ft.

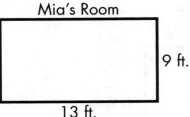

Mia's Room
9 ft.
13 ft.

Who will need more carpeting? _____ How much more? _____ sq. ft.

I found (perimeter, area) to solve the problem.

3. Diego is making a fence for his dog. He bought 176 feet of fencing. If his yard is 30 feet wide, how long can his fence be? _____

I found (perimeter, area) to solve the problem.

4. Alma is making a picture frame out of wood. She wants the frame to be one centimeter bigger than the painting all the way around. If her painting is 12 centimeters by 18 centimeters, how much wood does she need to get? _____
Draw a picture below to help solve the problem.

I found (perimeter, area) to solve the problem.

Area and Perimeter Word Problems

Solve. If needed, draw a picture.

1. An animal enclosure at the zoo is 8 meters wide by 12 meters long. How much fencing is needed to surround it? _____

2. If the area of a square table is 36 square meters, how long is each side of the table? _____

3. Rohan is making an enclosure for his rabbit. If he bought a plank of wood 48 inches long and wants to use all of it, what dimensions could his enclosure be? _____

4. Ms. Roberts is cutting carpet squares for her 9 kindergarteners to sit on. She wants each carpet square to be 24 inches long by 18 inches wide. How many square inches of carpeting does she need to purchase? _____

Name _____ Date _____

Line Plots

Use each line plot to answer the questions.

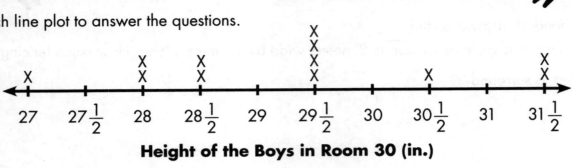

Height of the Boys in Room 30 (in.)

1. What is the difference in the height of the tallest and shortest boys? _____ in.

2. How many boys are $29\frac{1}{2}$ inches tall? _____

3. What height are the most boys? _____

4. How many boys are less than 29 inches tall? _____

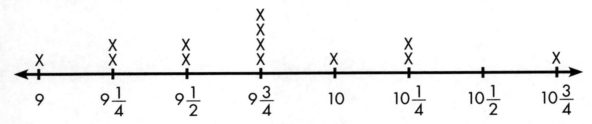

Age of the Girls in Room 30

5. What is the difference in the age between the oldest and youngest girls? _____

6. How many girls are younger than 10 years old? _____

7. Some more girls joined Room 30. Add them to the line plot.

Mariana: $9\frac{3}{4}$ Emma: 10   Maya: $9\frac{1}{4}$ Sofia: 9

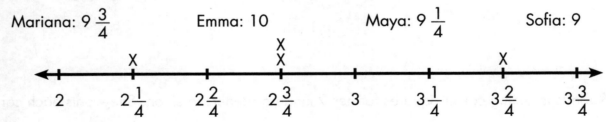

Miles Run by Running Club

8. What is the total amount of miles run? _____

9. How did you find the answer to problem 8? _____

_____

Angles

1. A 90° angle is what fraction of a circle?

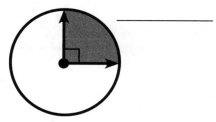 _____

2. A 180° angle is what fraction of a circle?

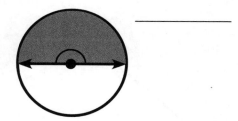 _____

3. A circle is made up of _____ one-degree angles.
   A. 90
   B. 180
   C. 360

4. An angle is made up of _____.
   A. a bent line
   B. two rays
   C. two line segments

Match the type of angle with its measure.

5. _____ an acute angle

6. _____ an obtuse angle

7. _____ a right angle

A. 90°

B. greater than 90°

C. less than 90°

Circle the most likely measurement of each angle.

8.

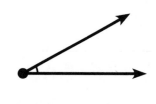

30°   90°   120°

9.

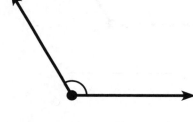

40°   90°   120°

10.

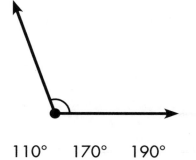

110°   170°   190°

11.

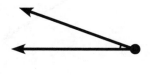

20°   50°   90°

Measuring Angles

Use a protractor to measure each angle.

1.

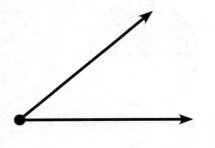

_____

2.

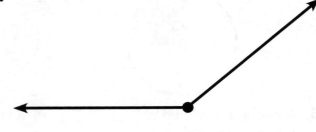

_____

3.

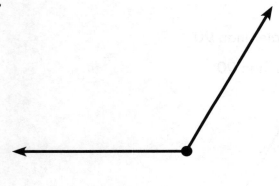

_____

4.

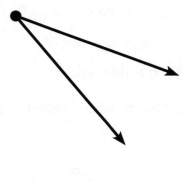

_____

5.

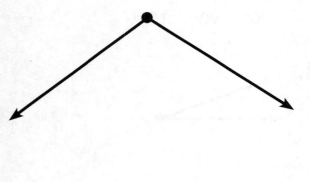

_____

6.

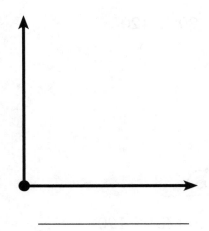

_____

Measuring Angles

Use these cards to assess students' ability to accurately measure angles. First, have a student sort the cards by whether an angle is less than, greater than, or equal to 90°. Then, have her measure each angle, using a protractor. If needed, add a self-stick note to the edge of a card to allow more space for extending a ray for measurement. If students are struggling, set out three different angles. Give the angle measurement of one of the three cards and have the student hold up the correct card.

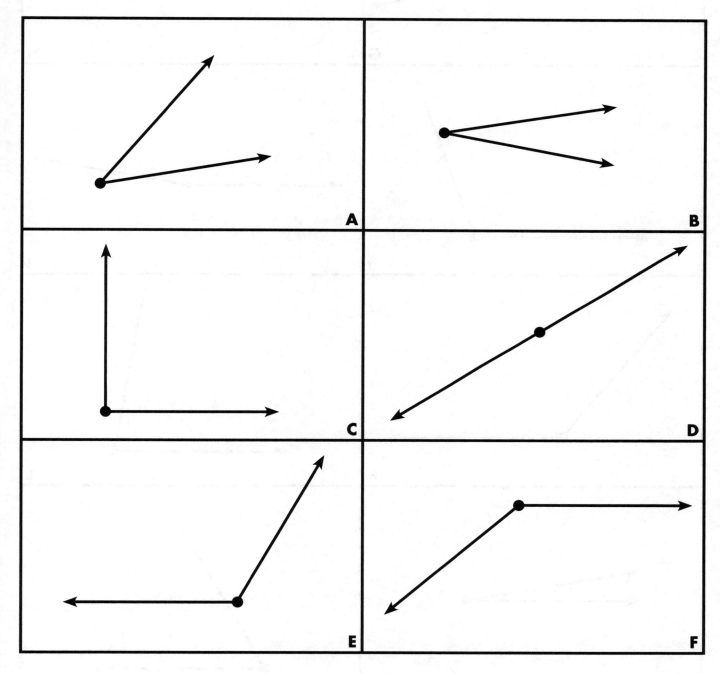

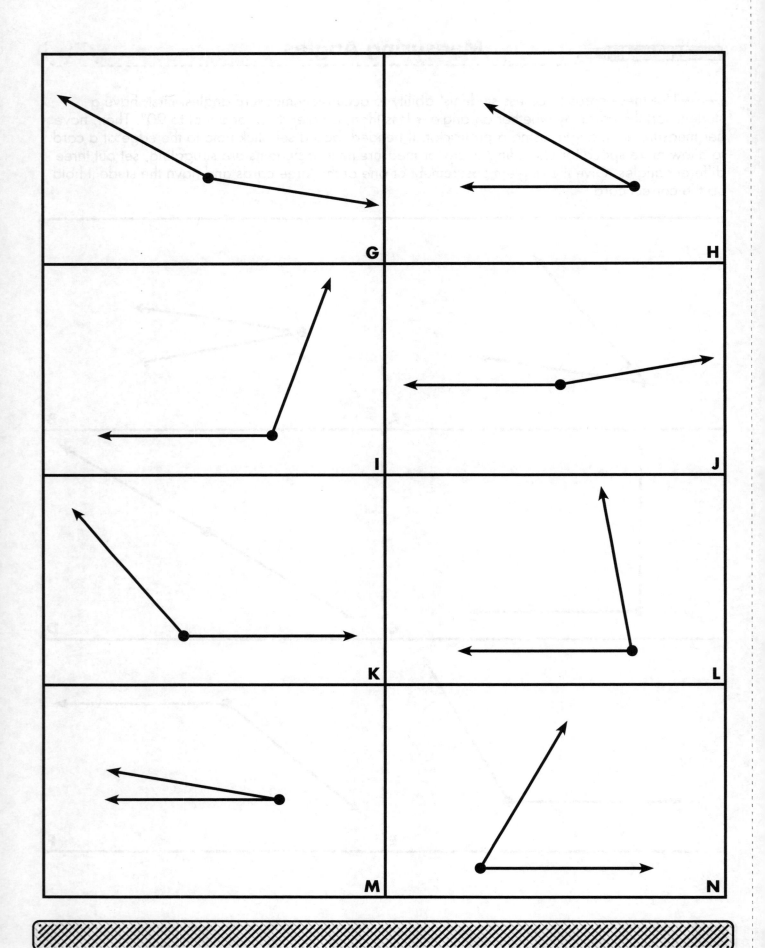

G

H

I

J

K

L

M

N

Name _____ Date _____

Drawing Angles

Complete each angle to match the measurement shown.

1. 40°

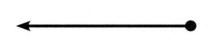

2. 80°

3. 120°

4. 170°

Draw an angle for each given measure.

5. 90°

6. 20°

Sums of Angles

Find the measure of each missing angle without using a protractor.

1.

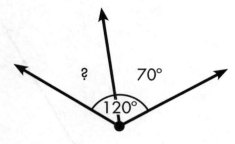

_____

2.

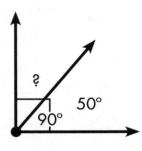

_____

3.

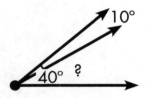

_____

4.

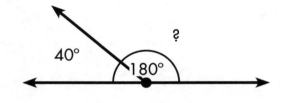

_____

5.

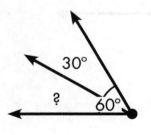

_____

6.

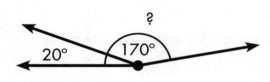

_____

7.

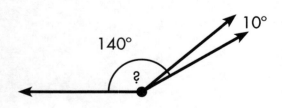

_____

8.

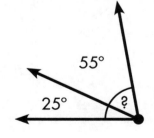

_____

A

Circle the largest unit of measure in each set.

kilogram   liter

gram   milliliter

minutes   centimeter

seconds   meter

B

Complete the table.

feet	yards
1	
2	
3	
4	
5	

C

Solve.

10 pounds = _____ ounces

7 kilograms = _____ grams

30 grams = _____ milligrams

30 pounds, 4 ounces = _____ ounces

D

Solve.

9 feet = _____ inches

3 meters = _____ centimeters

170 kilometers = _____ meters

10 kilometers = _____ centimeters

E

Solve.

5 hours = _____ minutes

40 minutes = _____ seconds

2 days = _____ hours

36 hours = _____ minutes

F

Use **<**, **>**, or **=** to compare.

9 kilometers ◯ 900 centimeters

1,500 grams ◯ 1 kilogram

70 liters ◯ 70,000 milliliters

G

Solve.

Mason has 24 quarters. His sister has $7. How many more quarters does he need to have as much money as his sister has?

_____

H

Solve.

A bag of russet potatoes weighs 3 pounds. A bag of sweet potatoes weighs 50 ounces.

Which weighs more? _____

How much more? _____

Find the perimeter.

6 ft.

2 ft.

P = _____

I

Find the area.

16 m

8 m

A = _____

J

Solve.
Beth's yard is 30 meters wide by 45 meters long. If she wants to add a fence around the entire yard, how many meters of fencing does she need? _____
The Carlsons' family room is getting new carpeting. If it is 16 feet by 24 feet, how many square feet of carpeting do they need?
_____

K

Use the line plot to answer the questions.

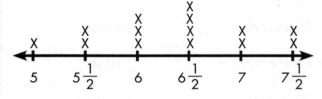

What is the largest size shoe worn? _____
What size do the most students wear? _____
Jamie wears a size 7 shoe. Add him.

L

Circle the most likely measurement of the angle.

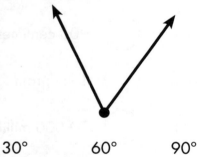

30°   60°   90°

M

Use a protractor to measure the angle.

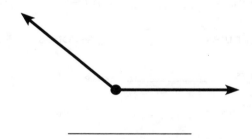

_____

N

Draw an angle to match the given measure.

40°

O

Find the measure of the missing angle.

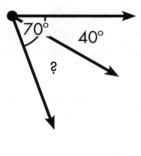

70°   40°

?

_____

P

Show What You Know
Geometry

Circle the correct name to match each picture.

1. ●━━━━━●

    A. line

    B. point

    C. ray

    D. line segment

2. ●━━━━━▶

    A. line

    B. point

    C. ray

    D. line segment

3. ◀━●━━━●━▶

    A. line

    B. point

    C. ray

    D. line segment

4. ●

    A. line

    B. point

    C. ray

    D. line segment

Label each angle as right (**R**), acute (**A**), or obtuse (**O**).

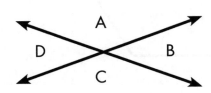

5. A. _____

    B. _____

    C. _____

    D. _____

6. A. _____

    B. _____

    C. _____

    D. _____

7. Circle the shapes that have parallel lines. Draw an **X** on the shapes that have perpendicular lines.

A.

B.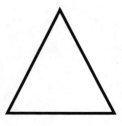

C.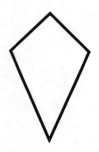

D.

Draw the line or lines of symmetry on each shape. Or, write **not symmetrical**.

8.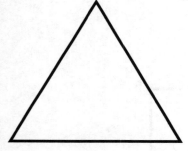

9.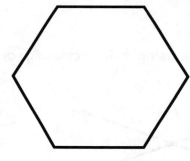

10.

11.

Name _____ Date _____

Show What You Know
Geometry

Write the letter of the picture that matches the word.

1. _____ point

2. _____ line segment

3. _____ line

4. _____ ray

5. _____ acute angle

6. _____ obtuse angle

7. _____ right angle

8. _____ parallel lines

9. _____ perpendicular lines

A.

B.

C.

D.

E.

F.

G.

H.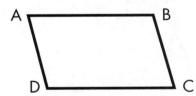

I.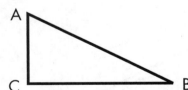

Label each angle as right (**R**), acute (**A**), or obtuse (**O**).

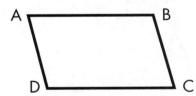

10. A. _____

B. _____

C. _____

D. _____

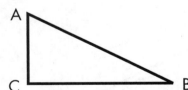

11. A. _____

B. _____

C. _____

12. Circle the shapes that have parallel lines. Draw an **X** on the shapes that have perpendicular lines.

A.

B.

C.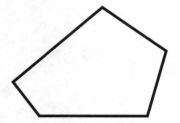

D.

Draw the line or lines of symmetry on each shape. Or, write **not symmetrical**.

13.

14.

15.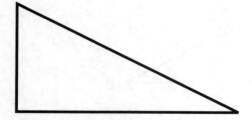

16.

Use the cards to assess whether students are able to classify shapes by a chosen property. Choose only one property to assess at a time, and have a student find all of the shapes that have that property. Properties to assess include right angles, obtuse angles, acute angles, parallel lines, and perpendicular lines.

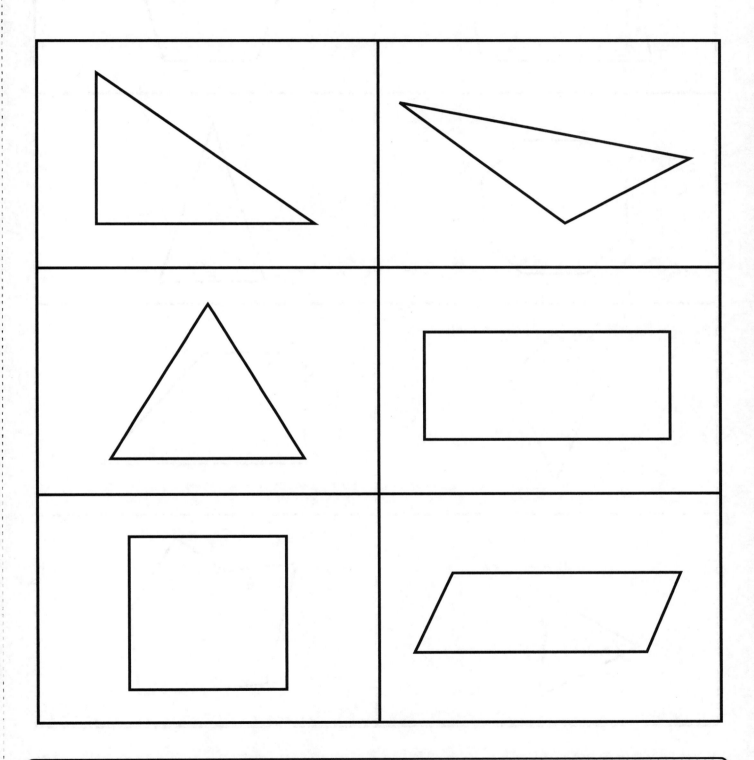

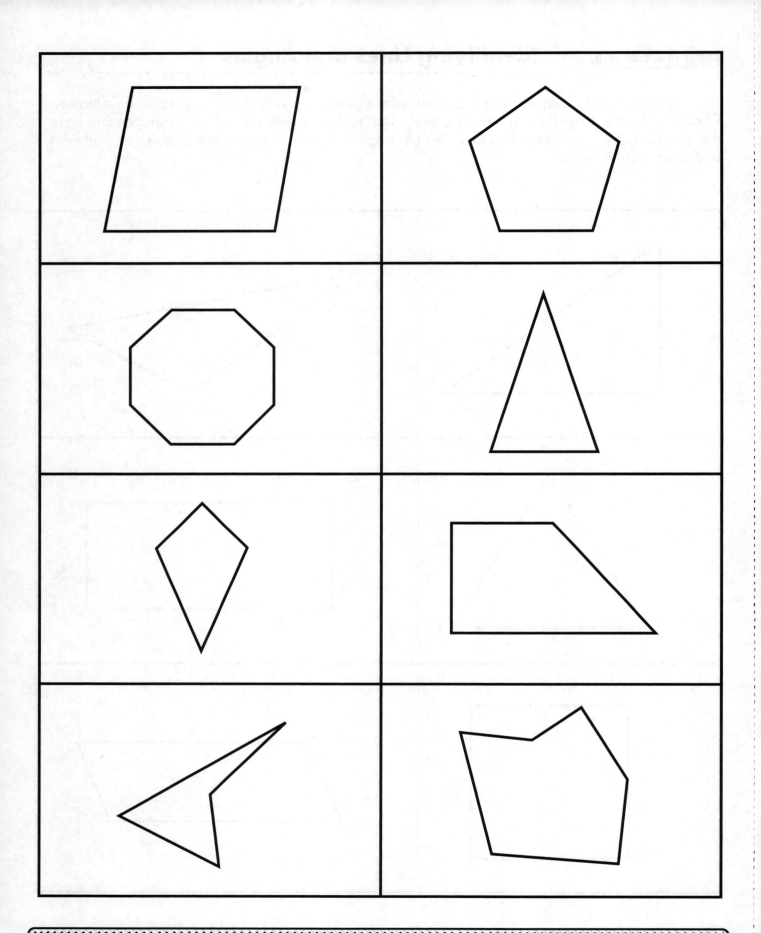

Name _____ Date _____

Geometric Terms

1. Draw a point.

2. Draw a line.

3. Draw a line segment.

4. Draw a ray.

5. How many lines are shown? _____

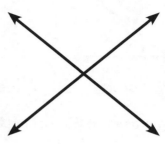

6. How many points are on a triangle? _____

7. Draw a shape that has 5 line segments.

8. What is the name of the shape you drew in problem 7? _____

9. How many angles are shown? _____

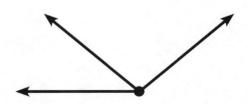

10. Trace each angle in problem 9 with a different color.

Types of Angles

Circle the type of angle shown.

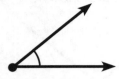

1. right   acute   obtuse

2. right   acute   obtuse

Label each angle as right (**R**), acute (**A**), or obtuse (**O**).

3.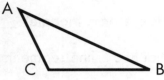

A _____
B _____
C _____

4.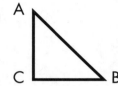

A _____
B _____
C _____

5.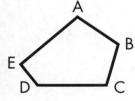

A _____
B _____
C _____
D _____
E _____

6.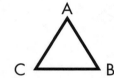

A _____
B _____
C _____

7. Draw a shape that has exactly 2 right angles. What shape did you draw?

_____

8. Draw a shape that has 2 acute angles and 2 obtuse angles. What shape did you draw?

_____

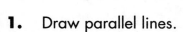

Parallel and Perpendicular Lines

1. Draw parallel lines.

2. Draw perpendicular lines.

3. Trace in red any parallel lines each shape has. Trace in blue any perpendicular lines each shape has.

A.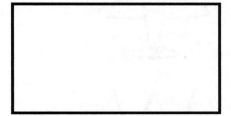

B.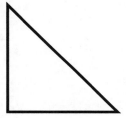

C.

D.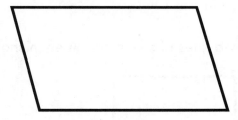

E.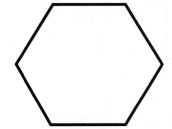

F.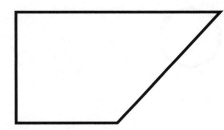

Lines of Symmetry

1. Circle the objects that are symmetrical.

A. 　　　　B. 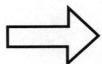　　　　C. 3

D. 　　　　E. 　　　　F.

Draw a line of symmetry on each shape.

2. 　　　　**3.**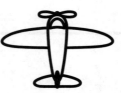

4. H　　　　**5.** W

Draw two lines of symmetry on each shape.

6. 　　　　**7.**

8. 　　　　**9.**

10. What is a line of symmetry? _____

_____

A

Draw and label a ray.

What is a ray? _____
_____

B

Draw and label a line segment.

How is a line segment different from a line?
_____
_____

C

How many points are there on a pentagon?
_____

How many line segments?
_____

How many angles?
_____

D

What kind of angle is shown? _____

How do you know? _____
_____

E

Draw an obtuse angle.

What is an obtuse angle? _____
_____

F

Label each angle as right (**R**), acute (**A**), or obtuse (**O**).

A _____   B _____

C _____   D _____

E _____

G

Circle the word that correctly completes the sentence.

A triangle can have 2 (right, acute, obtuse) angles.

Explain. _____
_____
_____

H

Circle all that are true.

A parallelogram can have (0 right angles, exactly 2 right angles, exactly 4 right angles).

Explain. _____
_____
_____

Draw a right triangle.

What makes it a right triangle? _____

_____

I

Draw a triangle with 1 obtuse angle and 2 sides the same length.

J

Draw a shape that has parallel lines. Circle the parallel lines.

K

Draw a shape that has perpendicular lines. Circle the perpendicular lines.

L

Draw a shape that has both parallel and perpendicular lines. Circle the parallel lines. Put an **X** on the perpendicular lines.

M

Draw a line of symmetry.

Name something that does not have a line of

symmetry. _____

N

Write 3 capital letters that are symmetrical. Draw the lines of symmetry.

_____   _____   _____

Write 3 capital letters that are not symmetrical.

_____   _____   _____

O

Draw two shapes that have more than one line of symmetry. Draw the lines of symmetry.

P

Answer Key

Page 11
1. $9 \times 4 = 36$; 2. $4 \times 5 = 20$; 3. Answers will vary. 4. 671 cans, $1{,}435 - 764 = 671$; 5. Arrays should include 1×6, 6×1, 2×3, and 3×2. 1, 2, 3, 6; 6. composite, It has factors other than 1 and itself. 7. 4: 4, 8, 12, 16, 20, 24, 28, 32; 6: 6, 12, 18, 24, 30, 36, 42, 48; 12, 24; 8. 8, 14, 20, 26

Page 12
1. $40 \times 5 = 200$; 2. $3 \times 4 = 12$; 3. Answers will vary. 4. 66 cards; $11 \times 6 = 66$; 33 cards each; 5. Arrays should include 1×20, 20×1, 2×10, 10×2, 4×5, and 5×4. 1, 2, 4, 5, 10, 20; 6. composite, It has factors other than 1 and itself. 7. 3, 6, 9, 12, 15, 18, 21, 24; 8, 16, 24, 32, 40, 48, 56, 64; 24; 8. 3, 5, 9, 17

Page 13
1. $4 \times 3 = 12$; 2. $12 \times 4 = 48$; 3. $5 \times 6 = 30$; 4. $6 \times 8 = 48$; 5. $6 \times 6 = \$36$; 6–8. Answers will vary.

Page 14
1. 8 pieces; $60 \div 7 = 8r4$; 4 left; 2. 22 shoes; $(7 \times 2) + (4 \times 2) = 22$; 3. 4 pizzas, Answers will vary. $(3 \times 10) \div 8 = 3r6$; 4. 30 min.; $(200 - 20) \div 6 = 30$; 5. 2 packs; $23 \times 5 \div 100 = 1r85$

Page 15
1. Arrays should include 1×10, 10×1, 2×5, and 5×2. 1, 2, 5, 10; 2. Arrays should include 1×13 and 13×1. 1, 13; 3. Arrays should include 1×2 and 2×1. 1, 2; 4. Arrays should include 1×12, 12×1, 2×6, 6×2, 3×4, and 4×3. 1, 2, 3, 4, 6, 12; 5. Answers will vary but should explain that the numbers used for the columns and rows in the arrays are the factors. 6. 1, 2, 4, 8

Page 16
1. even; 1, 2; prime; 2. odd; 1, 5; prime; 3. even; 1, 2, 4, 8, 16; composite; 4. even; 1, 2, 4, 5, 8, 10, 20, 40; composite; 5. odd; 1, 17, prime; 6. even; 1, 2, 4, 8, 16, 32; composite; 7. odd; 1, 3, 5, 9, 15, 45; composite; 8. odd, 1, 3, 9, 27; composite; 9. even; 1, 2, 3, 4, 6, 8, 12, 24; composite; 10. A number whose only factors are 1 and itself. 11. A number that has factors other than 1 and itself. 12–14. Answers will vary.

Page 17
1. 2: 2, 4, 6, 8, 10, 12, 14, 16; 5: 5, 10, 15, 20, 25, 30, 35, 40; 10; 2. 2: 2, 4, 6, 8, 10, 12, 14, 16; 3: 3, 6, 9, 12, 15, 18, 21, 24; 6, 12; 3. 5: 5, 10, 15, 20, 25, 30, 35, 40; 10: 10, 20, 30, 40, 50, 60, 70, 80; 10, 20, 30, 40; 4. 6: 6, 12, 18, 24, 30, 36, 42, 48; 20: 20, 40, 60, 80, 100, 120, 140, 160; none; 5. 7: 7, 14, 21, 28, 35, 42, 49, 56; 8: 8, 16, 24, 32, 40, 48, 56, 64; 56

Page 18
1. 3; 15, 18, 21; 2. subtract; 58, 50, 42; 3. 5; 107, 219, 443; 4. 2, 1; 63, 127, 255; 5. multiply by 2; 16, 32, 64; 6. 8, 13, 18, 23; 7. 33, 26, 19, 12; 8. 1, 1, 1, 1; 9. square; 10. star; it has 4 repeating shapes; 11. triangle; Answers will vary but may state that the 40th shape would be a star so it would be the shape before that. 12. Answers will vary but may state that the numbers are the multiples of 3.

Pages 19–20
A. $3 \times 8 = 24$; B. $4 \times 3 = 12$; C. Answers will vary. D. 4 batches; $48 \div 12 = 4$; E. 48 eggs; $12 \times 4 = 48$; F. 1×18, 18×1, 2×9, 9×2, 3×6, 6×3; 1, 2, 3, 6, 9, 18; G. 1, 2, 3, 4, 6, 8, 12, 24; H. 1, 2, 7, 14; I. composite; It has factors other than 1 and itself. J. 1, 2, 3, 5, 7, 11, 13, 17, 19; K. 15, 21, 25; L. 5: 5, 10, 15, 20, 25, 30, 35, 40; 6: 6, 12, 18, 24, 30, 36, 42, 48; 30; M. 72; N. 13, 16, 19, 22; add 3; O. 6, 16, 36, 76; P. 2, add 2, Answers will vary.

Answer Key

Pages 21–22
1. 10; 2. 100; 3. 10; 4. 700,000; 5. 10;
6. 0; 7. 5,626; 8. 904,716; 9. five hundred
nine thousand three hundred two;
10. 248,500, 250,000, 200,000, 248,500,
249,000; 11. <; 12. >; 13. =; 14. <;
15. 9,632; 16. 2,369; 17. Answers will vary.
18. 1,031; 19. 315; 20. 3,787;
21. 92,840; 22. 434; 23. 56,304;
24. 3,403; 25. 42,763; 26. 7; 27. 21;
28. 13r2; 29. 1,366r3

Pages 23–24
1. 1,000; 2. 10; 3. 1,000,000; 4. 20;
5. 200,000; 6. 3,000; 7. 11,845;
8. 291,301; 9. two hundred forty-five thousand
six; 10. 560,000, 563,790, 563,800,
564,000, 600,000; 11. =; 12. >; 13. >;
14. <; 15. 8,752; 16. 2,578; 17. Answers will
vary. 18. 1,998; 19. 63; 20. 35,802;
21. 36,382; 22. 715; 23. 1,512; 24. 1,943;
25. 16,416; 26. 10; 27. 144; 28. 873r5;
29. 1,216r1

Page 25
1. 10; 2. 100; 3. 100; 4. 10; 5. 40,000;
6. 1,000; 7. 60; 8. 1,000; 9. 10; 10. 900;
11. 80; 12. 20,000; 13. 400,000;
14. 1,000,000; 15. 6; 16. 530,006;
500,000 + 30,000 + 6; 17. twenty-four
thousand eight hundred fifty; 20,000 + 4,000
+ 800 + 50; 18. 549,242; five hundred
forty-nine thousand two hundred forty-two;
19. twenty-nine thousand four hundred eight;
20,000 + 9,000 + 400 + 8; 20. 390,283;
three hundred ninety thousand two hundred
eighty-three

Page 26
1. 25,400; 2. 2,400; 3. 14,900; 4. 10,000;
5. 17,400; 6. 52,700; 7. 40,000;
8. 850,000; 9. 30,000; 10. 10,000;
11. 390,000; 12. 470,000; 13. 685,470;
14. 685,500; 15. 685,000; 16. 690,000;
17. 700,000; 18. when the digit in the place
value to the right is 5, 6, 7, 8, or 9;
19. when the digit in the place value to the
right is 0, 1, 2, 3, or 4; 20. Answers will vary
but should include that you would look at the
thousands place value. Since it is 5 or above,
you would round the 3 to a 4 for an answer of
440,000.

Page 29
1. <; 2. >; 3. <; 4. >; 5. <; 6. <; 7. =; 8. >;
9. >; 10. 8,742; 11. 2,478: 12. Answers will
vary.

Page 30
1. 1,294; 2. 252; 3. 951; 4. 1,001;
5. 12,429; 6. 1,356; 7. 611; 8. 294;
9. 24,499; 10. 40,252; 11. 111,110;
12. 107,864; 13. 11,643; 14. 170,553;
15. 752,384; 16. 108,004; 17. 1,000,000;
18. 999,988; 19. 28,367; 20. 975,601

Page 31
1. 255; 2. 296; 3. 96; 4. 261; 5. 1,158;
6. 1,080; 7. 3,996; 8. 2,304; 9. 3,424;
10. 6,000; 11. 20,460; 12. 74,184;
13. 50,172; 14. 18,942; 15. 27,675

Page 32
1. 3,154; 2. 1,269; 3. 620; 4. 2,496;
5. 8,928; 6. 4,482; 7. 144; 8. 800;
9. 1,558; 10. 1,692; 11. 990; 12. 2,808;
13. 1,380; 14. 121; 15. 9,801

Page 33
1. 5; 2. 3; 3. 16; 4. 13; 5. 16; 6. 60; 7. 40;
8. 25; 9. 9r1; 10. 4r4; 11. 12r4; 12. 7r3;
13. 4r1; 14. 10r1

Page 34
1. 68r2; 2. 97; 3. 2,231r1; 4. 135; 5. 546r2;
6. 337; 7. 52r1; 8. 61r1; 9. 700r4;
10. 1,562r3; 11. 815r2; 12. 544

Pages 35–36
A. 10; 100; B. 10; 600; C. 6, 9, 3;
D. 704,562, 25,900; E. 400,000 + 80,000 +
3,000 + 900 + 80 + 4; F. 309,008;
G. three hundred forty-five thousand two
hundred seventy-five; H. 900, 3,900, 12,000,
46,000; I. 950,000, 948,000, 900,000,
948,100; J. >; >; <; K. 5,762, 19,918;
L. 2,882, 314; M. 3,984, 37,842; N. 2,494,
1,638; O. 31, 15; P. 23r1; 38r3; 534r1

Pages 37–38
1. 6; 2. 2; 3–4. Answers will vary. 5. Answers

will vary but may include $\frac{3}{6}$ and $\frac{4}{6}$.

6. Answers will vary but may include $\frac{3}{12}$ and

$\frac{4}{12}$. 7. =; 8. <; 9. >; 10. <; 11. $\frac{2}{3}$; 12. $\frac{6}{12}$;

13. $\frac{4}{6}$; 14. $\frac{84}{100}$; 15. 1, 4; 1, 4; 16. 3; 17. 6;

18. 2; 19. $4\frac{2}{3}$; 20. $16\frac{8}{12}$; 21. 8; 22. $10\frac{1}{6}$;

23. $\frac{3}{4}$ tsp; 24. $\frac{1}{6}$ of the marbles;

25. $4 \times \frac{1}{5}$; 26. $3 \times \frac{1}{10}$; 27. $\frac{6}{2}$ or 3; 28. $\frac{49}{10}$

or $4\frac{9}{10}$; 29. $\frac{3}{4}$ of a sheet of paper; 30. $\frac{6}{2}$ or

3 bags; 31. 40, 60; 32. 0.3, Check students'

work. 33. 0.58, Check students' work. 34. 0.3;
35. 0.51; 36. <; 37. <; 38. <; 39. =

Pages 39–40
1. 10; 2. 30; 3–4. Answers will vary.

5. Answers will vary but may include $\frac{3}{12}$ and

$\frac{2}{12}$. 6. Answers will vary but may include $\frac{3}{15}$

and $\frac{10}{15}$. 7. >; 8. <; 9. >; 10. >; 11. $\frac{6}{8}$;

12. $\frac{35}{100}$; 13. $\frac{6}{12}$; 14. $\frac{5}{10}$; 15. 4; 8; 16. 9;

17. 4; 18. 1; 19. $10\frac{4}{10}$; 20. $18\frac{7}{8}$; 21. $8\frac{2}{8}$;

22. $23\frac{3}{5}$; 23. $\frac{2}{4}$ of a mile; 24. $\frac{6}{8}$ of the trees;

25. $2 \times \frac{1}{5}$; 26. $7 \times \frac{1}{12}$; 27. $\frac{12}{5}$ or $2\frac{2}{5}$;

28. $\frac{21}{12}$ or $1\frac{9}{12}$; 29. 1 dowel; 30. $\frac{15}{4}$ or $3\frac{3}{4}$

cups; 31. 10, 20; 32. $\frac{29}{100}$; 33. 0.2, Check

students' work. 34. 0.53, Check students' work.
35. 0.8; 36. 0.57; 37. <; 38. >; 39. >; 40. <

Page 41
1–2. Check students' work. 3. 12;
4. 12; 5. 25; 6. 15; 7. 16; 8. 21; 9. 12;
10–16. Answers will vary. 17. Answers will
vary but should include how the numerator and
the denominator are multiplied by the same
number.

Page 42
1. $\frac{3}{4} = \frac{6}{8}$; 2. $\frac{2}{3} > \frac{3}{6}$; 3. $\frac{3}{8} > \frac{1}{4}$; 4. $\frac{7}{12} < \frac{2}{3}$;
5. >; 6. =; 7. <; 8. <; 9. >; 10. =;

11. >; 12. <

Page 46
1. X: $\frac{1}{4} = \frac{4}{8}$, $\frac{3}{4} = \frac{4}{12}$, and $\frac{1}{5} = \frac{2}{20}$;

2–8. Answers will vary. 9. >; 10. =;

11. <; 12. <

Page 47
1. $\frac{4}{5}$; 2. $\frac{6}{8}$; 3. $\frac{7}{10}$; 4. $\frac{4}{4}$; 5. $\frac{3}{6}$; 6. $\frac{7}{8}$;

7. $\frac{14}{10}$; 8. $\frac{9}{12}$; 9. $\frac{22}{12}$; 10. $\frac{110}{100}$; 11. $\frac{59}{100}$;

12. $\frac{76}{100}$; 13. $\frac{4}{3}$; 14. $\frac{6}{8}$; 15. $\frac{14}{10}$; 16. $\frac{14}{12}$;

17. $\frac{87}{100}$; 18. $\frac{57}{100}$

Answer Key

Page 48

1. $\frac{4}{8}$; 2. $\frac{2}{4}$; 3. $\frac{2}{6}$; 4. 0; 5. $\frac{7}{8}$; 6. $\frac{6}{12}$;

7. $\frac{4}{12}$; 8. $\frac{42}{100}$; 9. $\frac{10}{12}$; 10. $\frac{38}{100}$; 11. $\frac{1}{12}$;

12. $\frac{50}{100}$; 13. $\frac{45}{100}$; 14. $\frac{5}{8}$; 15. $\frac{1}{12}$; 16. $\frac{40}{100}$

Page 49

1. $\frac{1}{4}$; 2. $\frac{1}{6}$; $\frac{1}{6}$; 3. 2; 4. 4; 5. $\frac{5}{10}$;

6. 4; 7. 4; 8. 11; 9. 2; 10. 5, 2; 11. 1, 2;
12–16. Answers will vary.

Page 50

1. $5\frac{2}{3}$, Check students' work. 2. $3\frac{2}{4}$, Check

students' work. 3. $6\frac{2}{4}$; 4. $10\frac{6}{8}$; 5. $15\frac{8}{10}$;

6. $13\frac{3}{5}$; 7. 15; 8. $79\frac{66}{100}$; 9. $4\frac{2}{4}$; 10. $2\frac{2}{6}$;

11. $6\frac{8}{10}$; 12. $65\frac{2}{8}$; 13. $8\frac{4}{12}$; 14. $18\frac{67}{100}$

Page 51

1. $\frac{4}{5}$ of the pizza, Check students work.

2. $\frac{2}{4}$ of an hour; $\frac{4}{4} - \frac{1}{4} - \frac{1}{4} = \frac{2}{4}$; 3. $\frac{2}{4}$ cup;

$\frac{1}{4} + \frac{1}{4} = \frac{2}{4}$; 4. $\frac{6}{10}$ are black; $\frac{10}{10} - \frac{4}{10} = \frac{6}{10}$;

5. $\frac{9}{10}$ are yellow, blue, or orange;

$\frac{6}{10} + \frac{1}{10} + \frac{2}{10} = \frac{9}{10}$; $\frac{1}{10}$

Page 52

1. $3 \times \frac{1}{8}$; 2. $2 \times \frac{1}{5}$; 3. $4 \times \frac{1}{10}$; 4. $35 \times \frac{1}{100}$;

5. 1; 6. $\frac{2}{8}$; 7. $3\frac{4}{12}$; 8. 3; 9. 2; 10. $4\frac{2}{4}$;

11. 2; 12. $1\frac{3}{5}$; 13. 2 pizzas;

$5 \times \frac{1}{4} = \frac{5}{4}$; 14. yes; $1\frac{1}{5}$ miles; $6 \times \frac{1}{5} = \frac{6}{5}$;

15. 3 cups; $4 \times \frac{3}{4} = \frac{12}{4} = 3$

Page 53

1. 70; 2. 20; 3. 50; 4. 0.2, Check students'
work. 5. 0.6, Check students' work. 6. 0.78,
Check students' work. 7. 0.22, Check students'
work. 8. 0.34, Check students' work. 9. 0.4;

10. 0.7; 11. 0.58; 12. 0.02; 13. $\frac{65}{100}$;

14. $\frac{20}{100}$; 15. $\frac{68}{100}$

Page 54

1. >, Check students' work. 2. >, Check
students' work. 3. <, Check students' work.
4. <, Check students' work. 5. >; 6. >; 7. >;
8. <; 9. <; 10. >; 11. <, Check students' work.
12. >, Check students' work. 13. <, Check
students' work. 14. >, Check students' work.
15. <; 16. >; 17. <; 18. >; 19. <; 20. <

Pages 57–58

A. 6, 12; B. X: $\frac{1}{4} = \frac{4}{12}$ and $\frac{1}{6} = \frac{2}{3}$;

C. Answers will vary. D. 1. >, <, >, <; E. $\frac{4}{6}$;

$\frac{4}{10}$; $\frac{8}{10}$; $\frac{59}{100}$; F. 0, $\frac{4}{8}$, 0, $\frac{16}{100}$; G. $\frac{1}{8}$, $\frac{1}{8}$; 3;

8; 5; H. $8\frac{2}{5}$; $13\frac{5}{10}$; $15\frac{35}{100}$; I. 0;

$2\frac{2}{4}$; $\frac{1}{6}$; J. $\frac{2}{4}$ of a mile; $\frac{3}{4}$ cup; K. $6 \times \frac{1}{8}$;

$5 \times \frac{1}{12}$; L. $\frac{7}{8}$ cup; M. 90; 0.84; Answers will
vary. N. 0.8; 0.1; 0.33; 0.61; O. 1. >; 2. >;
3. <; 4. <; P. 1. >; 2. >; 3. <; 4. >

Answer Key

Pages 59–60

1. 8 kg; 2. 1 km; 3. 16; 32; 4. 60; 240; 5. 2; 10; 6. <; 7. =; 8. Her brother is taller. 9. 27 oz.; 10. $87; $116; 11. 18 cm; 18 sq. cm; 12. 80 ft.; 256 sq. ft.; 13. 84 m; 14. 120 sq. ft.; 15. Answers will vary but should include 1 × 24, 2 × 12, 3 × 8, or 4 × 6. 16. 5; 17. 19; 18. 30°; 19. 50°; 20–21. Check students' work. 22. 90°; 23. 50°

Pages 61–62

1. 5 lb.; 2. 1 kg; 3. 20; 80; 4. 100; 600; 5. 16; 160; 6. >; 7. <; 8. Pepper; 9. They have the same amount. 10. 3,000 m; 11. 16 ft.; 16 sq. ft.; 12. 26 m; 30 sq. m; 13. 266 cm; 14. 20 sq. ft.; 15. Answers will vary but should include 1 × 50, 2 × 25, or 5 × 10. 16. 2 ft.; 17. 17; 18. 140°; 19. 40°; 20–21. Check students' work. 22. 50°; 23. 60°

Pages 63–64

1. no; 2. 129 oz.; 36 in.; 4. $\frac{1}{3}$ of a foot; 5. 2,000 mL; 6. 90 min; 7. 4,000 m; 8. $1\frac{2}{4}$ lb., 4 lb.; 9. $\frac{1}{4}, \frac{1}{10}, \frac{1}{20}, \frac{1}{100}$; 10. 3 in., 1 in.; 11. 21 days; 12. yes, yes; 13. $156; $195; $117; 14. Bruce; Answers will vary but should explain how the numbers were converted into the same unit of measure.

Page 65

1. 1 L; 2. 2 m; 3. 5 ft.; 4. 20 kg; 5. 60 min.; 6. 1 lb.; 7. mm, cm, m, km; 8. sec., min., hr.; 9. 10, 20, 30, 40, 50; 10. 12, 24, 36, 48, 60; 11. 32; 12. 180; 13. 5,000; 14. 96; 15. 60,000; 16. 300,000

Page 66

1. 28 ft.; 2. 30 in.; 3. 8 mm; 4. 20 cm; 5. 5 ft.; 6. 3 cm; 7–9. Answers will vary.

Page 67

1. 32 sq. in.; 2. 4 sq. ft.; 3. 40 sq. km; 4. 4 sq. cm; 5. 3 cm; 6. 18 ft.; 7–9. Answers will vary.

Page 68

1. 348 cm, perimeter; 2. Cole, 3 sq. ft., area; 3. 58 ft., perimeter; 4. 64 cm, perimeter

Page 69

1. 40 m; 2. 6 m; 3. Answers will vary but should include 2 × 24, 3 × 16, 4 × 12, or 6 × 8. 4. 3,888 sq. in.

Page 70

1. $4\frac{1}{2}$ in.; 2. 4 boys; 3. $29\frac{1}{2}$ in.; 4. 5 boys; 5. $1\frac{3}{4}$ years; 6. 9 girls; 7. Check students' work. 8. $11\frac{1}{4}$; 9. Answers will vary.

Page 71

1. $\frac{1}{4}$; 2. $\frac{1}{2}$; 3. C; 4. B; 5. C; 6. B; 7. A; 8. 30°; 9. 120°; 10. 110°; 11. 20°

Page 72

1. 40°; 2. 140°; 3. 120°; 4. 30°; 5. 110°; 6. 90°

Pages 73–74

A. 40°; B. 20°; C. 90°; D. 180°; E. 120°; F. 140°; G. 160°; H. 30°; I. 110°; J. 170°; K. 130°; L. 80°; M. 10°; N. 60°

Page 75

1–6. Check students' work.

Page 76

1. 50°; 2. 40°; 3. 30°; 4. 140°; 5. 30°; 6. 150°; 7. 150°; 8. 80°

Answer Key

Pages 77–78
A. kg, L, min., m; B. 3, 6, 9, 12, 15; C. 160, 7,000, 30,000, 484; D. 108, 300, 170,000, 1,000,000; E. 300, 2,400, 48, 2,160; F. >; >; =; G. 4 quarters; H. the sweet potatoes, 2 oz. more; I. 16 ft.; J. 128 sq. m; K. 150 m, 384 sq. ft.; L. $7\frac{1}{2}$, $6\frac{1}{2}$, Check students' work. M. 60°; N. 140°; O. Check students' work. P. 30°

Pages 79–80
1. D; 2. C; 3. A; 4. B; 5. O, A, O, A; 6. R, R, R, R; 7. circled: A, B; X: A, B, C; 8–11. Check students' work.

Pages 81–82
1. B; 2. G; 3. I; 4. E; 5. F; 6. D; 7. C; 8. A; 9. H; 10. A, O, A, O; 11. A, A, R; 12. circled: B, D; X: B, C; 13–16. Check students' work.

Page 85
1–4. Check students' work. 5. 2; 6. 3; 7. Check students' work. 8. pentagon; 9. 3; 10. Check students' work.

Page 86
1. acute; 2. obtuse; 3. A, A, O; 4. A, A, R; 5. O, O, O, O, R; 6. A, A, A; 7. Check students' work. Answers will vary but may include a pentagon or a trapezoid. 8. Check students' work. Answers will vary but may include a parallelogram or a rhombus.

Page 87
1–3. Check students' work.

Page 88
1. B, C, D; 2–9. Check students' work.
10. Answers will vary but should explain that it is an imaginary line that divides something into two identical parts.

Pages 89–90
A. Check students' work. a figure with one endpoint that continues in one direction; B. Check students' work. a line with two endpoints; a line continues in both directions; C. 5, 5, 5; D. acute; Answers will vary but should explain that it measures less than 90°. E. Check students' work. Answers will vary but should explain that it is an angle that measures more than 90°. F. A, O, R, R, O; G. acute; Answers will vary but should explain that it is not possible to have a three-sided shape with two right or obtuse angles. H. 0 right angles, exactly 4 right angles. Answers will vary. I. Check students' work. Answers will vary but should explain that it has a right angle. J–N. Check students' work. O. Answers will vary but should include A, B, C, D, E, H, I, K, M, O, T, U, V, W, X, or Y. Answers will vary but should include F, G, J, L, N, P, Q, R, S, or Z. P. Check students' work.